Hugh Seymour Tremendeere

A Manual of the Principles of Government as Set Forth by the Authorities of Ancient and Modern Times

Hugh Seymour Tremendeere

A Manual of the Principles of Government as Set Forth by the Authorities of Ancient and Modern Times

ISBN/EAN: 9783337267353

Printed in Europe, USA, Canada, Australia, Japan

Cover: Foto ©Suzi / pixelio.de

More available books at **www.hansebooks.com**

A MANUAL

OF THE

PRINCIPLES OF GOVERNMENT,

AS SET FORTH BY THE AUTHORITIES OF ANCIENT
AND MODERN TIMES.

BY

HUGH SEYMOUR TREMENHEERE, C.B.,

*Late Fellow of New College, Oxford, M.A., and of the Inner Temple,
Barrister-at-Law.*

"The basis of the philosophy of man is to be laid in the records of his past existence."—
HALLAM'S *History of Literature*, Vol. ii, p. 69.

A NEW AND ENLARGED EDITION.

LONDON:
KEGAN PAUL, TRENCH & CO., 1, PATERNOSTER SQUARE.

1882.

LONDON:
PRINTED BY ROWORTH AND CO. LIMITED,
NEWTON STREET, HIGH HOLBORN.

PREFACE.

THE First Edition of this book was published in 1852, the second in 1865, under the title of "The Political Experience of the Ancients, in its bearing upon Modern Times," and has been long out of print.

It comprised in its Second Part a summary of the opinions of a few of the greatest modern writers on the principles of government.

On republishing it, with considerable additions to the Second Part, it has been necessary to give it a more general title.

PART I remains as it was first published. In it I have put together concisely all that is most valuable in the treatises on politics that have been left to us by three of the most distinguished writers of antiquity.

Aristotle's celebrated treatise on government (commonly called his treatise on "Politics") was written after a careful investigation of all the constitutions under which the different free states of antiquity had been governed previously to and during his day.

The masterly sketch by Polybius of the rise and progress of the Roman institutions—the Preface to his great work on Roman History—was written at the time when the constitution had attained its greatest perfection.

The beautiful fragment of Cicero, "On a Republic," recovered in a remarkable manner in the year 1822 at Rome, contains a clear and philosophical exposition of a portion of the same subject, intermingled with touches of patriotism and of eloquence that give it an additional value.

These three dissertations embody nearly the whole of the "ancient wisdom" on the subject of constitutional government; and, notwithstanding the achievements of modern knowledge, are still recognised as the fountain head of the principles of Political Science, and as lights for the instruction of all ages. In the words of Burke, "The science of government would be poorly cultivated without the study of the form and spirit of the ancient republics."

In PART II, I have traced the current of philosophical opinion on the principles of government from the date of Cicero's treatise to the present day. It will be seen that this current runs through a series of great authorities, nearly all in substantial agreement on first principles, and all combining to exemplify the unity of history. I have thus endeavoured, in this compilation, to fulfil an intention expressed in the First Edition. My duties on many Parliamentary and Royal Commissions of Inquiry relating to the manufacturing, mining, and agricultural populations, from 1839 continuously to 1870,—with a view to the remedial legislation gradually adopted during those years and to the great measure of elementary education,—very early led me to believe, from the facts of a more general nature disclosed by those inquiries, that a short manual on the principles of government would be a useful and acceptable aid towards the formation of political opinion. I venture to think that its republication at the present time, with additions, will not be out of place.

CONTENTS.

PART I.

ARISTOTLE (B.C. 384—322) ON POLITICAL SOCIETY AND GOVERNMENT.*

	PAGE
Book I.—Origin and Objects of Political Society	1
II.—The Constitutions of the Free States of Greece	6
III.—The Franchise	10
The Different Forms of Government	12
IV.—The Progressive Changes of Government	24
The Conditions necessary to the Best Form of Government	38
V.—Of Revolutions	46
VI.—Of True Liberty	67
VII.—The Foundation of Public Happiness	70
On National Character	74
On Education	76

POLYBIUS ON THE ROMAN CONSTITUTION, IN THE PREFACE TO THE SIXTH BOOK OF HIS HISTORY OF ROME ... 78

EXTRACTS FROM CICERO'S TREATISE ON A REPUBLIC OR COMMONWEALTH ... 87

---

* The text which I used was that of Goettling, Jena, 1824.

PART II.

OUTLINE OF THE COURSE OF OPINIONS ON THE BEST FORM OF GOVERNMENT FROM THE DATE OF CICERO'S TREATISE TO MODERN TIMES.

	PAGE
† Introduction	119
† Machiavelli	120
† Bodin	123
° Bacon	126
† Bellenden	129
Harrington	131
Algernon Sydney	132
† Locke	134
° Vico	143
° Hume	146
° Montesquieu	149
° Dugald Stewart	152
° Pitt, Fox, Burke	158
Sir James Mackintosh	177
° Earl Russell, John Stuart Mill, and other authorities on the Representation of Minorities	181
° John Stuart Mill on Bentham	199
° De Tocqueville on the Omnipotence of Majorities	203
° Earl Russell on Representation	205
° Postscript	208

* The subjects marked with an asterisk, and all the passages in the text between brackets [ ], have been added in the present edition; those marked † have been rewritten.

APPENDIX.

° A.—M. De Tocqueville and other authorities on the Old Government of France and the Revolution ("L'Ancien Régime et la Révolution") ... 211

° B.—The Change, within the last fifty years, of the Constitutions of the individual States of the American Union to pure Democracies, and its effects on the General Government 227

° C.—The Origin and Growth of our Constitution, from the earliest Records of History 259

* The subjects marked with an asterisk have been added in the present edition.

THE PRINCIPLES OF GOVERNMENT.

PART I.

ARISTOTLE

ON POLITICAL SOCIETY AND GOVERNMENT
(B.C. 384—322).

BOOK I.

Objects of Political Society.—Various Forms of.—Origin and Growth of.

ERRATA.

Page 126, line 14, for "have" read "who have."

Page 163, line 24, for "other power" read "the other powers."

Page 203, line 25, for "138" read "139."

Page 214, last line, insert comma after "resolutions."

Page 223, line 6, for "de d'y voter" read "d'y voter."

Page 225, first line, for "equally" read "Equally."

Page 242, line 6, for "before the public" read "to light."

In order to do so, let us look at society in its growth.

ERRATA.

Pag: 126, lin: 14, for "give", read "who have".

Pag: 130, lin: 24, for "other power", read "the other."

Pag: 213, lin: 25, for "183," read "133."

Pag: 214, lin: 1ult, insert comma after "ros latlos."

Pag: 223, li: 5, for "du d'y voiles" read "d'y voler."

Pag: 237, line 1ino, for "otura'y," read ", H pa'tra,"

Pag: 311, line 6, for "boé in a'tra ta'tilo," read "a'tra."

THE PRINCIPLES OF GOVERNMENT.

PART I.

ARISTOTLE

ON POLITICAL SOCIETY AND GOVERNMENT
(B.C. 384—322).

BOOK I.

Objects of Political Society.—Various Forms of.—Origin and Growth of.

EVERY political society is a sort of community or partnership; and as every partnership is established for the sake of some good, apparent or real, expected to result from it, it is plain that the greatest partnership of all, presiding over and comprehending all the rest, namely, a commonwealth or political society, must aim at the greatest good and the highest benefits that can be derived from such a union.

The forms which commonwealths or political societies assume are various, and to understand them aright we must analyse them, and resolve them into their constituent elements.

In order to do so, let us look at society in its growth.

We shall there find that certain parts or elements, which cannot exist separately, are brought together by a mutual necessity, namely, males and females; for without this union the species would cease to exist.

In the same manner, also, unless some ruled and others obeyed, society would be destroyed; for there would be no security, and consequently society would perish.

The same necessity, therefore, that compels association produces government.

Again, knowledge and foresight are requisite for the safety of a community. There must, therefore, be the head to devise and to rule, and the hand to obey and execute. And hence the relation of master and servant.

Of the associations above mentioned, that of the Family is the first in order; as says Hesiod (B.C. 850), "Get first a house, and then a wife, and then an ox to plough;" for this primary association is founded on daily exigency.

The next, founded, not on daily exigency, but on the occasional requirements of mutual utility, is the association of many houses, or the Village.

The village seems to have arisen naturally as the offshoot or colony from the family; as is indeed denoted by the name given to it in some places, where the village is called a community, "nourished by the same milk," the children and grandchildren of the original stock.

Now, as every house is ruled by the head of the

family, and as these several families in the village belonged to the same stock, and recognised the same original head, their relationship led them to obey that head. And thence arose the principle of obedience to a chief or king; which principle was by degrees extended from the village to a collection of villages, to a city or a commonwealth, and thence to nations.

This was the opinion in the time of Homer (B.C. 1000), for he says: " To wives and children patriarchs gave the law;" for the growing communities were, as it were, of a man's own household.

The village community having in the course of its growth provided for its natural wants, the next step therefore is, that out of the union of many villages is formed a city or commonwealth. As the object of the village community is to provide the means of existence, the object of the union of many villages into a city or commonwealth is to protect, exalt, and perfect that existence. And this end and aim of a commonwealth or political society is as conformable to nature, as the end and aim of the earlier and simpler associations. For that which conduces to the perfection of a thing is most in accordance with the order of nature. Man is therefore as much formed by nature for a state of political society, as he is for the simplest bonds of union—those of his family and his village. Even some animals unite in a sort of society, and have the means of communicating to each other their pains and pleasures; but to man alone has been given the power of considering and giving expression to what concerns him—what is good or bad for him; what is expedient or hurtful; just or unjust. And in order to consider these things in common, men unite and form themselves into a political society. They do so, as it were, by a natural impulse, for they perceive that it leads to the perfecting of man's nature. For without law and justice man is the worst of all creatures. For, first of all, he has craft and courage; he then furnishes himself with arms, and uses them against everything right and good; he becomes the embodiment of armed injustice, which is the cruellest of tyrannies. Unholy and savage, knowing nothing of religion, virtue, or law, he abandons himself to his passions, to lust and gluttony. Numerous were the benefits, therefore, that he conferred on mankind, whoever he was, who first taught men to live together in political societies. As the whole is greater than a part, so is society greater than an individual; and as a hand or foot can hardly be properly called such, in reference to their uses, if separated from the body, so an individual is as nothing, apart from the society to which he belongs. For if he could stand alone and apart from all his fellows, so might all the rest; which is unnatural and impossible for man.

Political society, therefore, is a greater and loftier thing than an individual, and prior even in the intention of Nature; for Nature (or the God of Nature) intended, not man's existence alone, but the perfecting of his moral and intellectual being, which is impossible except under the protection of political society, of which justice is the rule and basis.

Aristotle (Chapters 2 to 5) then proceeds to analyse the different domestic relations, which consist of husband and wife, father and child, and, in his time, of master and slave. We need not follow him in his reasonings in favour of the institution of slavery, the mild and enlightened spirit of Christianity having extinguished it among civilized nations; or in the details of the remainder of this Book, the subjects touched upon belonging chiefly to the province of political economy, and being, therefore, now better understood. After pointing out the different means by which, in the early growth of society, the industry of the individual and the family contributed first to their support, and then to the increase of their wealth and substance, he adds:—

" The next step in the social progress is that of the interchange of commodities, and, in order to facilitate this, the use of money. Thence arose the love of gain, and, by degrees, the pursuit of wealth for its own sake, the passion of avarice ever strengthening itself in the mind. Mere accumulation becomes in that case the end and aim of existence, instead of the endeavour to improve and embellish existence by the cultivation of all the moral and intellectual qualities. This passion of money-getting is in itself boundless, and if it cannot satisfy itself by fair means, it does not scruple to resort to others, prostituting the best powers and principles to its service. Very different from this inordinate passion is the moderate and equitable pursuit of wealth, with a view to comfortable subsistence and a provident care for those that are to come after us. This is consistent with the development of every virtue; and it should ever be borne in mind, in all reasonings and all measures having the increase of wealth for their object, that there is a greater thing than that to be considered; namely, the cultivation of virtue and the elevation of man's nature. And this is the work of Education, a subject deserving of every attention; for its first object is to develop the domestic virtues; and on the domestic virtues depend those of the state."

BOOK II.

Having thus traced the growth of society from its infancy, Aristotle proceeds, in his Second Book, to investigate the different forms of government known in his time, in order to determine which was the best. It is said that, in order to qualify himself for this task, he studied the laws and constitutions of two hundred commonwealths.* Cicero bears testimony to the fact, that Aristotle in this work "expounded the manners, institutions, and social arrangements of nearly all the existing states; not those of Greece only, but those of all the neighbouring countries."†

Ideal Commonwealths and their Errors.—Sketch of the Constitutions of Sparta, Carthage, and Athens, their Excellences and Defects.

Before entering upon these, however, he disposes of the arguments adduced in his day in favour of Plato's imaginary Republic, founded on a community of wives, children, and property. He shows such an arrangement of society to be contrary to nature, destructive of industry and enterprise, as well as of all the natural affections, and consequently rendering impossible all social and moral progress, and all virtue. He then notices other schemes of ideal republics; first, that of Phaleas of Chalcedon, who proposed the equalization of property.‡ But to

---

* Fabricius, Bibliotheca Græca. Hamb., 1791, vol. ii, p. 196, quoted by Dr. Gillies, in his translation of the "Politics," in 2 vols. 8vo, 1804. This translation gives Aristotle's work entire, and, therefore, contains much that is now useless with reference to modern times; it contains also long dissertations that have a strong party bias.

† De Finibus, Lib. v, c. 4.

‡ Modern socialism and communism are scarcely more than the reproduction of these errors, which were exploded upwards of 2,000 years ago.

this Aristotle objects that, even if it were desirable, in order to make it effectual a restraint must at the same time be placed upon marriage, and also upon education; for otherwise the increase of numbers, and the free development of the faculties of those gifted with superior ability, would soon destroy that equality. Neither would such equality conduce to greater happiness or greater order and tranquillity; for it would not extinguish in the human mind either its passions and ill-regulated desires, or its ambition, which, if it has not a natural and equitable course open to it, will gratify itself at any risk and by any means, even the most violent, and end in the subversion of the state. The real remedy for these passions, and the most effectual means of happiness, are to be found, he says, in industry, in the cultivation of the mind and heart, and in the pursuits of wisdom and philosophy.

Chapter 5.—He next deals with the ideal commonwealth proposed by Hippodamus, the architect who constructed the Piræus; and having shown the fallacy of its pretensions, he warns his countrymen against rash innovations generally, as tending to weaken the authority of law.

"Many," he says, "go so far as to doubt the expediency of changing the ancient laws even for those that may be better. But in this they are wrong; for it is impossible that every state of circumstances can have been foreseen from the beginning, and it is necessary, therefore, that legislation should adapt itself to a new condition of things. But these changes should be effected with great care and caution, and it is better to bear with some amount of error and inconvenience rather than accustom men lightly to change the laws and institutions of their country. For these laws and institutions derive a great portion of their efficacy from time and custom, and lightly to change them weakens the habit of obedience, and undermines the authority of all law."

Chapter 6.—Having as it were cleared the ground, by noticing the various forms of ideal republics which were attracting attention in his time, he takes in hand four of the most conspicuous commonwealths known to the Greeks, the Spartan, the Cretan, the Carthaginian, and the Athenian; and of these respectively he points out the characteristic faults and excellences. In the Spartan he comments on the poverty of the magistrates (the Ephori), elected to represent the people. This poverty exposed them to bribery, and subjected them to the influence of demagogues.

"Yet," he adds, "imperfect as was this institution, it contributed to the duration of the Spartan government; for in it all classes were represented: the kingly power; the aristocratic, whose talents and virtues placed them in the senate; and the democratic, acting through their elected magistrates: all orders of the state, therefore, were satisfied with its arrangements, and harmoniously combined together to preserve it."

After adverting to other defects in the Spartan institutions, and especially that their main scope and object was the cultivation of the warlike at the expense of all the other virtues, he passes in review the government of Crete, which was earlier and more imperfect than that of Sparta. (Chapter 7.) In that of Carthage, which is similar in its general character to those of Crete and Sparta, he finds more subjects of commendation; the proof of its good qualities being, that, under it, order and liberty had been preserved for many generations.

"It had, however," he says, "one conspicuous fault, that of giving too great weight, in the selection of its principal public officers, to mere wealth, irrespective of mental cultivation, sense, and virtue. Than this, there can scarcely be a greater source of evil, as leading a whole nation to the immoderate love of gain and the worship of money; for when this is encouraged by the institutions of a country, and by the heads of the community, the opinion and feeling is speedily caught up and followed by the whole body of the people, and leads inevitably to the corruption both of the governing body and the governed. It is a reproach to the laws of any country, if they do not give full and fair scope to the development of wealth and well-being, and thence to those opportunities of leisure which enable well-disposed and able men to devote themselves to public duties, and to whatever may benefit their country; but to prefer mere wealth to cultivation, to character, and to capacity to discharge those duties well and faithfully, is base and corrupting, and will bring about by degrees the ruin of any community, under whatever form of government."

Chapter 9.—With striking brevity, in one short page, Aristotle proceeds to analyse, to exhibit the faults, and to relate the fall of the Athenian constitution. The narration seems to be in harmony with the brief and brilliant career of this the most remarkable people of antiquity. Writing within a comparatively short period of the greatest epoch of their glory, while their name still filled the world, while their passions which their ambition had provoked were still unallayed, and the ruin it had brought upon the whole of Greece was still fresh and palpable, it is worthy of observation with what complete philosophic calmness this "wisest of the ancients" explains in a few words the principles of Solon's institutions, and points out the two or three fatal errors afterwards engrafted upon them, which caused their overthrow.

He says: "Solon is thought to have judiciously mingled the different elements of the Athenian constitution, by giving the oligarchical its due weight in the Areopagus, the aristocratical in the magistracies, and the popular in the judicial body. And in giving this share of power to the people, he only did what was fair and equitable; for, without the power of electing their magistrates[*] and calling them to account for their administration, there can be neither liberty nor contentment in a state. But this popular power was by degrees unduly extended; and, after encroaching upon, it finally extinguished, all the rest. For first Ephialtes and then Pericles curtailed the powers of the Areopagus. Pericles again, and other demagogues after him, by paying the people for the discharge of their public duties, introduced corruption, which went on increasing, under the influence and by the intrigues of successive demagogues, until it ended in the present democracy. And for this change it does not seem that Solon or his institutions are in fault so much as the dispositions of the people; for, after their great naval victories and their success in war, they became unduly elated, and chose as their magistrates bad and corrupt men, who conducted the affairs of the state after their own manner, and, consequently, brought it to its present condition."

Aristotle then touches lightly upon some few constitutions of other states of Greece, or of the countries connected with it, but reverts to the fact that those above described are the only ones of which it is necessary to give the details.

BOOK III.

Definition of a Citizen.—Privilege of full Citizenship, how obtained.—What Portion of the Community ought to be invested with Political Power.

The Third Book opens with an inquiry into the proper definition of the word citizen. In the opinion of Aristotle—

---

[*] In modern times "representatives."

"The answer to this question is different in different states, and depends on the laws and constitution of each. The whole body of the inhabitants of a country enjoying the protection of its laws—including the young, who are still under the legal age, and the very old, who have passed the time of action, and all others under any other species of disability—are, in a certain wide and general sense, citizens. But the full and complete definition of a citizen is confined to those who participate in the governing power, either by themselves or their representatives. This privilege is not attached to mere residence in a place or country, or derived from descent; for the question always recurs, how did the original possessor obtain it? It is a privilege conferred in a legal manner by the act of the state. Sometimes it has been greatly extended by a revolution in the government, as by Cleisthenes, when the Tyrants were expelled from Athens; and in that, and similar instances, it admits of doubt, whether it was rightly or wrongly extended to so many strangers and persons in a servile condition; but the fact remained, and those on whom power was then conferred retained it. He who is entrusted with this privilege in a democratic government is, more than others, invested with the powers of a citizen. And the number of citizens so invested with a portion of the governing power in a state ought to be sufficient to ensure all the purposes of security and well-being for which society was founded."

Chapters 2 and 3.—The second and third chapters treat of the question, whether the virtues of a good man and a good citizen are the same; an inquiry with respect to which the strict and comprehensive rules of Christian morality can leave no doubt. It is, therefore, unnecessary to follow Aristotle's argument on this point. One observation which he makes in the course of it is, however, worthy of remark; namely, that while it is the especial duty of those who govern, to seek to arrive at wisdom and truth, it is no less the duty of the governed to endeavour to form a right judgment of the acts of their rulers; which cannot be done without cultivation and study. It was this opinion which led to the exclusion, in many of the ancient commonwealths, of artizans and all who were obliged to gain their living by the work of their hands, from all participation in the governing power; for it was thought that moral and intellectual cultivation, and the capacity of forming a right judgment, could not be expected when the faculties were absorbed in the drudgery of manual labour. In some states, the superior classes of artizans were admitted to the rank of full citizenship, as being supposed to have acquired wealth, and, therefore, leisure. In others, a political necessity, such as a want of population, induced them sometimes to admit strangers, and even persons of servile condition. But Aristotle's opinion, formed on the ancient condition of society, is against the admission of artizans, and even of all freemen who were not above the necessity of manual labour. His argument in this chapter, as throughout his whole work, treats the question of admission to full citizenship, and to a consequent participation in the governing power, as one to be determined by the circumstances of each community, with reference to the good of the whole. The facilities of acquiring knowledge, and the means of elevating the moral character, even in the humblest grades of life, in the present day, so different from anything that Aristotle was acquainted with, render his strict limitations as to classes now inapplicable, without, however, affecting the principle so clearly worked out wherever he touches upon the origin of the wisest and best arrangements of political power; namely, that they do not flow from any abstract rights in individuals, but from a just and enlightened sense of expediency in each particular case, having in view the safety of the state, and the best interests of the community.

On the Different Forms of Government.

Chapters 4 and 5.—We have now to consider carefully the different forms of government, their distinctive characters, and the ends and objects of each.

It has been shown that men's instincts lead them to form themselves into political societies for the enjoyment of social life, for mutual protection, and for the improvement and embellishment of existence. The object, therefore, of all good government is, the pursuit of the common good. This object, however, is aimed at by institutions differing from each other in form and principle; each of which may, nevertheless, under the existing circumstances, be a good government. There is, for instance, the government of one individual; there is another form, where the government is in the hands of a few; a third, where it is in the hands of a great number. When the One, the Few, or the Many govern well, and for the common good, theirs must be called a good government. But if they govern with a view to their own particular interests, that is a corruption, and becomes a selfish and a bad government. A just and good government in the hands of one man we call a Monarchy; a just and good government in the hands of a few we call an Aristocracy, either because the best men conduct the state, or because they rule with a view to the best interests of the whole; and when the many, consisting of all orders united, govern for the common good, we call that by the general name of a Polity, or Republic, or mixed government.* And these names are justified by experience; for the highest qualities for government are often found in

---

* So denominated by Aristotle in speaking of Lycurgus's Constitution for Sparta.

one man, or in a few. But the tastes and qualifications of the many incline towards the warlike virtues; and citizens who are soldiers have usually a large share of power in a republic. The corruptions of these forms of government are—a tyranny from monarchy, an oligarchy from an aristocracy, and a democracy from a well-arranged polity or republic. A monarchy becomes a tyranny when the monarch governs with a view to his own exclusive interests; an aristocracy becomes an oligarchy when the interests of all other classes are sacrificed to the wealthy few; and a republic becomes a democracy when the interests of all other classes are sacrificed to what appears most conducive to the interests of the poor; while, in all, the general good is overlooked, or deemed a second consideration. For this reason none of these corruptions are endurable. For the object of government is not to increase the wealth of the few, nor to favour the poor at the expense of the rest, nor to encourage mere equality; nor is it established for mutual defence alone, nor for the promotion of trade and commerce only, nor for any other exclusively material purpose; but its greatest and highest end and aim is, to make virtuous and good citizens; to promote the happiness arising from blamelessness of life; to lead to the perfecting of man's social and moral nature; and to encourage those great and noble deeds that dignify and adorn one's country. Those, therefore, who can most contribute to all these results, have the best title to a share in the government.

Chapter 6.—In what portion of the state, therefore, ought the sovereignty to reside? It has been seen that all the simple forms of government are liable to fall into the abuses peculiar to each, and to work injustice to some section of the community. It has been accordingly said, that for these reasons the law, and not individuals, should be the ruling power. But what if the law be in its spirit despotic, or oligarchical, or democratical; wherein will it differ from a tyranny without law? The simple forms, therefore, are to be avoided. But of all the modes of government, there is a probability that the one in which the people at large (including all orders) have the chief power, will be the best; for some communities may be sufficiently instructed and cultivated to use such power wisely, while others, on the contrary, are as little fit to be entrusted with it as wild beasts. The probability that some communities would in fact use such a power wisely, arises from the circumstance, that the people collectively often come to sounder conclusions than they would have done as individuals; for they have the opportunity of hearing the best opinions on any subject of deliberation, and of enlightening each other. Moreover, it is the best plan to admit to a participation in the governing power as many as can be admitted with safety; for where large numbers are excluded, there will be discontent and danger. Solon, guided by this principle, judiciously assigned to the people at large the power of electing the magistrates, and calling them to account for their administration. He thought them capable collectively of discharging this duty with sufficient discrimination; and when thus acting in union with the best and most enlightened citizens, they confer great benefits on the state by their joint councils; just as, in matters of diet, a union of several ingredients is the most wholesome, the coarse and the fine being judiciously blended together. And although it may be objected, that to entrust such important functions to the mass of the people is like giving credit to the patient for a greater knowledge than the physician, or placing the pupil above the master; yet it must be remembered, that as he who inhabits the house is a better judge of its comfort than the architect who built it, so those who are most affected by laws and institutions are the quickest to appreciate their merits or to feel their defects.*

Chapter 7.—Who, then, are the persons best entitled

---

* Solon's constitution was founded on property. "He divided the citizens into four classes, according to the gradations of their fortunes, and regulated the extent of their franchise, and their contributions to the public necessities, by the amount of their incomes." (Thirlwall's History of Greece, vol. ii, p. 37.) The four classes were: 1st. Those whose estates yielded a net yearly rent of 500 medimni ($\pi\epsilon\nu\tau\alpha\kappa\sigma\sigma\iota\circ\mu\acute{\epsilon}\delta\iota\mu\nu\sigma\iota$). The medimnus equalled one bushel and six pints. 2nd. The Knights ('Ιππεῖs) who were able to keep a horse and to serve as cavalry. 3rd. The small farmers using one yoke of oxen (Ζευγῖται). 4th. Smaller proprietors and labourers in husbandry (Θῆτες). The two latter classes formed the infantry of the state; those of the fourth class being also liable to be called upon to man the fleet.

Whether any others than those engaged in husbandry were included in the Θῆτες does not appear, either from Solon's classification, or from Aristotle's comments on it. But, in praising Solon's constitution, it is clear from the course of his argument, in B. ii, c. 8, and in B. iii, c. 3, that he considered one of its chief merits to consist in its being founded on property.

to be entrusted with the administration of public affairs? Not the mere rich alone, or the mere noble alone, for those qualities are accidental, and imply no special ability for the discharge of public duties. Moreover, when riches alone, or birth alone, are allowed to be the only claim to power, the government quickly degenerates into an oligarchy. In the same manner, if personal superiority is taken as the basis, then the argument leads to the selection of one individual, and therefore to a tyranny. But to every citizen qualified by education and good conduct, the road to honour and power should be open; and no state is well or wisely governed where this is not the case. Where it is so, there the laws are framed with a view to the best interests of the whole body of the community; and those who frame or administer, as well as those who are called upon to obey them, fulfil their respective duties as good men and good citizens.

Ostracism.

Chapter 8.—A law here calls for observation, which is found chiefly in democracies. The natural endowments and the opportunities of men being different, some will greatly exceed the rest in all great and good qualities, and consequently in political influence. But, as the principle of democracies is equality, states under that form of government have adopted the practice of Ostracism, or sending into banishment any of their citizens who greatly excel the rest in wealth, influence, or any other species of political power. Tyrants and oligarchies also adopt the same mode as democracies in getting rid of or keeping down superior citizens. But all these, being perversions of good government, do this with a view to the particular interests of individuals or classes in the state. No such law exists among any people whose government aims at the general good of the whole body of the people. A government ought to be so constituted as not to want such a mode of protection; for, notwithstanding all palliative measures, such a power is generally used unjustly.

Nevertheless, under a really good government, which embraces all classes under its protecting care, what, it may be asked, is to be done with those citizens who overtop the rest in wealth and influence, and in all good and valuable qualities of mind and conduct? Clearly no sensible man would say that they should be banished. The obvious thing to do is, at all times to give them their due weight in the national councils, as the persons best qualified as natural rulers to direct the state with a view to the good of all.

Kingly Power.—Various Changes from, to other Forms of Government.—The Law should be supreme in all.

Chapter 9.—The above observation naturally leads us to speak of Kings. We have already said that monarchy is one of the just forms of government. There are, however, various kinds of monarchy. There are kings who, like the Lacedæmonian, are mere generals for life; there are hereditary and elective monarchs, and there are the Asiatic kings, who are nearly unlimited in their power, which is supported by the laws and customs of their country, and by the servile disposition of their people. There were also, in the earliest times in Greece, kings invested with absolute power by the free will of the people, sometimes chosen for life, sometimes for a particular exigency.

Another species of monarchy prevailed in the heroic ages, that of an hereditary loyalty, limited by law, and maintained by the willing obedience of the people. It arose from the circumstance of the first founders of it having been the benefactors of their people, either in war, or by the useful arts, or by having led the way in colonizing a new country; they received, therefore, a voluntary submission from public gratitude. They became generals in war, and judges in peace, and presided over such religious ceremonies as did not belong to particular priesthoods. This perpetual presidency over the domestic affairs and foreign relations of their subjects they lost by degrees—by voluntary surrender in some instances, by the act of their people in others—until, in most states, the kingly office is now reduced to a mere superintendence of religious matters, except in Sparta, where it has become only a military command.

An inquiry arises, whether it is best to be governed by one individual of superior wisdom and virtue, or by the best laws. The answer is, that it is best to be governed by good laws, with the best men in the state to administer them. When too much power is given to one man, too much scope is left to human weakness and human passions.

These are more apt to be kept in check when the governing power is in the hands of many, provided security is taken that they be men duly qualified for the exercise of it,—that they be, as far as possible, men of good principles, of mature age and experience, and possessed of the full privileges of citizenship.

States have generally begun with Monarchy, as in small communities they seldom found more than one man fit to govern. But as the number of good and able men increased, they proceeded to what was preferable, namely, an Aristocracy, and set on foot a "Polity," or institutions having in view the common good. Becoming corrupt, however, through the increase of wealth, the governing body plundered the community, and, contracting power into a few hands, they degenerated into an Oligarchy. And this arose from wealth being too much an object of pursuit.

The next step was to the tyrannical government of one or a few, and after that to a Democracy; for the usurping factions continually narrowing the basis of their power, in the corrupt pursuit of their own interests, provoked the mass of the people, and gave them spirit and strength to overcome their rulers, and to set up a Democracy. And, indeed, when communities become very large, it is, perhaps, difficult for any other than a democratic form of government to exist.

With respect to Monarchy, another question arises;

namely, whether it ought to be hereditary? It is possible that a bad prince may succeed a good one. In order, therefore, to prevent the ill effects that might arise from this contingency, it is right that the king should be invested with military power sufficient only for the support of the laws, but not enough to enable him to act arbitrarily and to oppress the community.

An unlimited monarchy appears to some unnatural; and indeed it is so in communities of freemen, among whom it is preferable that the law should govern, rather than any individual; and if any are invested with authority, it should be as guardians and administrators of the law, and as its just and wise interpreters. He who submits to law, submits to what has about it something of divine; but he who submits to the unlimited authority of man, submits to what may have all the passions of a wild beast; for evil desires and corrupt passions are apt to turn aside even the best rulers; but law is like a high intelligence, above the reach of passion.

It may be said, that if an individual is particularly skilled in the art of governing, he ought to be allowed to govern, just as you trust implicitly to a physician in matters relating to his art and science. But the physician has no object in view but that of doing his duty and curing his patient; whereas he who wields political power is constantly liable to be misled by personal feelings, by likes and dislikes, and by fear or favour. The safest plan, therefore, in political matters is, that the law, which aims at establishing the just mean between conflicting interests, should be supreme; especially that great moral law which is superior to the written, and to which all written laws ought to conform.

Besides, it is impossible for one man to conduct all the affairs of government. He must call in many to assist him. Is it not better, therefore, to provide for this in a legal and formal manner, and to make arrangements by which the administration of the country would be placed in the hands of a sufficient number of good and able men, capable of conducting it with a view to the common good?

We have now shown that there is a state of society in which the patriarchal mode of government is wise and natural; another, to which a monarchy is suitable; a third, in which men are fitted for living in what we have called a just and equal polity, in which all classes are represented, and which is administered with a view to the general interests. But tyrannies, whether of one man, or of an oligarchy, or of a democracy, are contrary to nature, and are corruptions of the just forms of government. These just forms, we have seen, are three; each suitable to the particular circumstances of the people; a monarchy, where the people are in a state to submit willingly to the ascendancy of one man, gifted with high personal qualities and with skill in the art of governing; an aristocracy, where the mass of the people are disposed to yield b edi ence to a certain number who have skill to govern well, and personal and political qualities that make them fit to govern freemen; and a polity or commonwealth, in which the conflicting powers of the state are united by their institutions, in such wise, that while all obey, any one may rise to power, according to laws that do not favour wealth only, but open the road to power to any who can by desert attain to it.* And where one man or a few are so much above the mass as to be alone capable of governing, in such a case he or they should neither be put an end to nor banished, but allowed to govern.

To recapitulate: we say, that there are three just forms of government, and of these, the best is that which is administered by the best men, under the particular circumstances of each; namely, that in which some individual, or class, or member, excelling in virtue, or highly qualified for power, bears rule; some submitting willingly to authority, some exercising it, and both having in view the highest ends of life. And since the virtue of the man is coincident with the virtue of the citizen in the freest and best state, it is plain that in the same way, by the same means, will be formed good men and citizens, both in an aristocracy and a monarchy. It is education and habit that make the good man and at the same time the just government, whether it be a

---

* This, the "Polity" of England, has been lately described by M. Lamartine as the true "Patrician Republic" of antiquity, with additions and perfections to which no ancient government attained.

constitutional government or an absolute monarchy. It remains for us to consider which of the three just forms is the best.

BOOK IV.

Practical Statesmanship.

The physician, in the exercise of his art, consults the varying constitutions of his different patients; the professor of gymnastics considers the different degrees of strength and aptitude of his pupils; in the same manner the political philosopher must adapt his speculations, not to a community that may by possibility be provided with all external and internal advantages, but to men as they are generally found, and to communities under a great variety of circumstances. For the statesman is not always able to adopt the measure which appears to his judgment to be clearly the best, but is obliged to put up with that which circumstances enable him to carry; and he is bound to look, not to the present only, but to the stability and duration of his country's institutions. He must observe what is fitting for men in general, and not stickle for what is theoretically the best; he must aim at what is possible and easily accomplished and most generally acceptable, and not follow the example of those who are never content but with some fancied perfection, or a state of things which can only arise under particular, and those very favourable, circumstances, like the Spartan constitution, and some others, which such men are always holding up to admiration. It is not an easier matter to renovate a constitution than to found one; just as it is sometimes as difficult a task to unlearn as to learn.

In order that the statesman may act beneficially under the varying circumstances of different constitutions, it is necessary that he should see clearly that there are many forms of democracy, and many of aristocracy, as well as of the other modes of government, and that his business is to discover and determine what is best and most fitting under the peculiar conditions of each; for a "Polity" or mixed government is an equitable arrangement for the distribution of power and the establishing of government, and holding up before the eyes of the citizens the chief end to be aimed at in political and social life.

Causes of the Progressive Changes of Government.

Chapter 2.—In our first classification of governments we laid it down that there were three just forms—a Monarchy, an Aristocracy, and a Polity or Commonwealth; and that there were three corruptions of these, namely, a Tyranny, an Oligarchy, and a Democracy. Of all of these there are many varieties, though called by the same name; some better for the governed, some worse; and the worst are generally those which arise from the corruption and degradation of what had been the best; as, for instance, a tyranny from a paternal monarchy, and a democracy from a well-regulated commonwealth.

An oligarchy is in principle always bad, but in practice some may be less bad than others. Now, when we have clearly set forth the differences of these various forms, and how each comes to be established, and how one may be preferable under one set of circumstances, and another under another, we shall be in a condition more fully to understand the essential principles of each, and to see what changes would be fatal and what would contribute to their well-being and preservation.

Chapter 3.—The cause of there being many forms of government is this. Each state consists of a great diversity of constituent parts. First, every community whatsoever is composed of a certain number of families. Of these, some are wealthy, some are poor, and some are in a middle condition between the two. Again, these same classes are engaged in various occupations; some subsist by agriculture, as owners, occupiers, or day labourers; some by trade and commerce; some by manual labour, as artizans. Of the upper classes, some are distinguished by birth, by their abilities, and by their virtues; some by their wealth only. In some forms of polity all these constituent elements of society have some share in the government; in others, a few only have it; in others, again, the number is extended beyond the few. And accordingly, as the constituent parts differ from each other, so will the governments differ, and take their form from the particular parts which have the leading influence in each. The most manifest and most specific difference is between riches and poverty, and, according as either of these two elements preponderates in a community, the tendency is for the government to incline either towards an aristocracy or towards a democracy. The truest and best forms are, as we have said before, two: a well-mixed and harmonized aristocracy; and the polity or commonwealth, which we have described, consisting of all orders and ranks, participating fairly in the governing power. These degenerate, the one into a highly-strung and despotic oligarchy, the other into a relaxed and self-indulgent democracy.

That there should be these different degrees and distinctive elements in society, is consonant with reason, and in analogy with every other form of existence. All animals have their distinctive and necessary parts, their peculiar senses and instincts, their organs of motion, their means of taking and receiving food: all these differ in different animals, in kind and in degree, but all are essential for each, to enable them to fulfil their respective functions. So it is with commonwealths. One portion of the people is employed in providing food; another in various arts and manufactures, some essential to existence, others valuable for the comfort and embellishment of life. There is then the large class engaged in trade and commerce. There are also those whose occupation it is to cultivate the art of war, an employment not less necessary than any of the foregoing, if a state would be secure from being conquered by any that may choose to attack it; for no commonwealth is worthy of the name, that has lost its military spirit and is not ready at once to defend itself and to repel aggression. There must be also judges and magistrates; for as the soul is superior to the body, so the means of self-defence and of administering justice are of higher importance than those arts which merely minister to our physical wants. Next to these is the occupation of the statesman, which is one requiring political wisdom. Suitable men are also required to fill all the various administrative offices; and if the state is to be well and honourably governed, such men must have the proper political knowledge, together with ability and integrity. But the most marked and palpable distinction of ranks is that of the rich and the poor; the first comparatively few, the latter comparatively numerous; and according as either of these bodies get completely the upper hand, the government is either an oligarchy or a democracy.

Chapter 4.—The persons of note in a community are distinguished by birth, wealth, education, virtue, and various good qualities. But democracy exists by, and aims at, equality; for the law of a democracy declares that the wealthy shall have no privileges above, or different from, the poor, nor have any title to be at the head of affairs any more than the poor; therefore, as the poor are the most numerous, and the opinion of the greatest number is paramount in such a society, a democracy is the government of a numerical majority. A second kind of democracy requires some qualification in point of property, though a small one, in those who would aspire to take part in public affairs. A third kind excludes all who have been found guilty of any offence. A fourth opens the way to all without distinction or limitation. But all these are governed by general and fixed laws. There is, however, another form of democracy in which the numerical majority is absolute, and general and fixed laws not respected, but occasional decrees take their place. This happens when the community falls under the hands of demagogues. In a well-ordered democracy demagogues have little weight, but the best citizens possess the seat of authority. Where the fixed laws or institututions are weakened, demagogues step in, and the people become despotic, like one individual monarch armed with absolute power. Both these despotisms are alike in nature and character; both have their flatterers; both are inclined to depress and set aside their best citizens; the one governs by decrees, the other by ordinances; and as flatterers rule tyrants, so demagogues lead democracies. The opinion of the majority is without check or control, and as demagogues wield that opinion, and draw everything under the cognizance and jurisdiction of that majority, they rule as they will, and pass what decrees they please. Again, demagogues invite the multitude to take all public offices into their own hands; the many are not backward to accept the invitation, and thus all established authority is destroyed. Such a state of things is unworthy the name of government.

Chapter 5.—Of oligarchies, also, there are many kinds. One confines political power to those only who have a certain income, and that is placed so high as to exclude the great body of the people. In another kind, the qualification for office is low, but the magistrates themselves fill up, by election, the vacancies in their own body; but if they elect from the great body of the citizens, and not from a small number possessing a certain income, they are rather an aristocracy than an oligarchy. In a third, offices are hereditary. In a fourth, in addition to offices being hereditary, the holders of them govern arbitrarily, and not according to fixed law; this form, therefore, which is called in Greece a "Dynasty," bears the same relation to aristocracy as tyranny does to monarchy, and democracy to a well-ordered commonwealth.

Revolutions worked silently by Changes of Manners or Habits.

It should, however, be observed, that very frequently a state may not, according to its fundamental laws, be democratic, and yet it may be governed democratically; and again, a state may be democratical in its laws, and yet be governed oligarchically. In these cases, manners and practice are at variance with theory. And this happens during periods of revolution. The changes do not take place suddenly; but while the new ideas are gaining ground, there is a lingering attachment to the old. The ancient laws preserve for a long time a nominal ascendancy, but in the end manners and habits prevail, and those who effected the change remain masters of the commonwealth.

To what People the Cheapest Form of Democracy is suitable.—Other Forms of Democracy.

When a people subsists chiefly by agriculture, and possesses only a moderate subsistence, it usually adopts a code of laws simple in themselves, and requiring little time or trouble in their administration; for such a people are obliged to work for their livelihood, and have little leisure to give to public matters. All who possess the amount of qualification required by law, are allowed to take a part in the assemblies, and are eligible for office; and as there is no payment for exercising these public duties, there is little competition for them, as those who exercise them must be able to live on their own resources.

In two other states of society a simple democracy of a similar kind may prevail. One where descent or birth, the other where mere citizenship as a freeman, qualifies for all offices; but where there are no salaries or fees for discharging public duties, few covet them, and the regular action of law is not interfered with.

The fourth species of democracy, and the last in point of time in the gradual development of communities, arises with the growth of wealth, and the consequent ability of the state to pay for public services. With the increase of population, and the gradual expansion of political power, the multitude finally gets the upper hand, and then insists on receiving payment for discharging public duties. A commonalty of this kind, living upon the public pay, and having no private business to attend to, have nothing to do but to frequent the assemblies and the courts of justice, which the wealthy abandon to them, so that all the powers of the state fall by degrees into the hands of the needy multitudes, who have no respect for established laws, but proceed to govern in accordance with their own notions.

The Various Forms of Oligarchy.

The first form of oligarchy is that founded on wealth and substance as the qualification for sharing in the government; and this being participated in by a numerous body possessing the requisite qualification in various degrees, is on the whole equitably administered. But when wealth accumulates in few hands, then the second form of oligarchy arises; for these few, strengthening themselves in the government by electing their own colleagues and partizans, turn their power to their own purposes, under the cloak, nevertheless, of law. But if their ambition increases, and they aim at accumulating still greater wealth and power in the hands of a few, they then proceed to possess themselves of all the branches of government and pass laws rendering their power hereditary as well as absolute. They are able next with ease to set themselves above the law, and thus this last form of oligarchy corresponds with the last and most corrupt form of democracy.

Of the Various Kinds of Aristocracy.

Besides monarchy, oligarchy, and democracy, there are two other forms of government: that which is called an aristocracy, and that which we have named by the general appellation of all commonwealths, a polity or mixed government; but this last, on account of its rare occurrence, has been overlooked by Plato and other writers on politics. Strictly speaking, and according to the definition we have already given, an aristocracy is purely and simply a government of the men most distinguished for worth and virtue; a government in which the duties of a good man and a good citizen exactly coincide. Some few oligarchies and some few commonwealths approach to this standard, inasmuch as honours and offices are in them conferred not alone with reference to wealth, but to worth, ability, and virtue. And a commonwealth in which this habit prevails in respect to the selection of men for public trust, is in a certain sense, and in that respect, an aristocratic commonwealth. For in all states there will be a certain number of men in all ranks of life, bearing high characters, and possessing distinguished ability; and the government that avails itself of these, and, as that of Carthage, seeks for its supporters among the wealthy, among those who are conspicuous for their moral qualities, and among the people at large, that government is an aristocracy.

In Sparta, worth and excellence, together with numbers, long shared the government. These, then, are the various forms of aristocracy; and we may add to these, every form of commonwealth in which the balance inclines to the side of the few.

The Mixed Form of Government, or the Aristocratic Commonwealth.

Chapter 6.—It remains to speak of the mixed form of government, or of a commonwealth properly so called. We have shown that neither the aristocracies which we have spoken of, nor the oligarchies, nor the democracies, and least of all the absolute government in the hands of one individual, are just forms of polity, or anything else than corruptions; but, by exhibiting their real nature and character, we are better able to place in a strong light what is the fairest and the best form of government.

It will be borne in mind that it has been above stated that the characteristic quality of a democracy is freedom, that of an oligarchy wealth, and that of an aristocracy virtue, or rather, more properly speaking, those intellectual and moral qualities which arise from cultivation, for which wealth and leisure afford the opportunity, and for which men are apt to give credit to those who possess such opportunities of acquiring them. It is assumed also, that men of virtue, ability, and wisdom, will pass good laws; that obedience to the law is recognised as the duty of a good citizen; and that the majority who enact the laws will cause them to be respected.

Now the union of these several qualities and characteristics—the freedom of a democracy, the wealth of an oligarchy, the intellectual and moral qualities, the high birth and breeding, of an aristocracy (for birth and breeding are the representatives of the wealth and virtues of past generations)*—forms what is best deserving the name of a government, and may be called distinctively an Aristocratic Commonwealth.

How such a Government may be formed, and how preserved.

Chapter 7.—We will now show how such a government may be formed and preserved. In the first place, give full scope and opportunity of exercise to the peculiarities of each form; let what is distinctive of a government in the hands of a few (such as the unpaid magistrates of Greece) exist in full vigour, and at the same time adopt into the system some of the principles and practices of a democracy. The blending of these opposite qualities will produce a mean between the two, and is therefore wise and politic. Again, it is politic to adopt the mean between what either party, when left to itself, enforces; as, for instance, an oligarchy raises the qualification for public office, or for taking part in public affairs,

---

* Ἡ γὰρ εὐγένεια ἐστὶν ἀρχαῖος πλοῦτος καὶ ἀρετή.

to a very high point; a democracy will have none, or a very little. Now neither of these is conducive to the common good of all, and is to be avoided; but a qualification intermediate between the two extremes is the proper one. So also as to the mode of election; a politic government, such as the aristocratic commonwealth we are describing, will borrow something of the peculiarities of both. The test of the admixture of all the elements being well and completely made, is, when a government may be called both aristocratic and democratic, according to the impression it makes on the person describing it. For both elements exist in its composition, and each appears most conspicuous according to the particular point of view from which it is regarded. Such is the Spartan government; and accordingly, by some who look to a certain portion of its institutions, it is called a democracy, while by others, who fix upon other portions, it is denominated an oligarchy. A mixed government, therefore, partaking in due proportions both of democracy and of oligarchy, should, at the same time, appear both and neither. It must also be able to maintain itself, without external aid, by its own native vigour; and it will do so as long as all its component parts are so well disposed that neither of them wish for any other form of government.*

---

* In Aristotle's criticism on Plato's Republic and Book of Laws, in the Second Book of the "Politics," he points out, among other matters, that Plato has not clearly explained what he means by mixed government, and intimates that he omits the aristocratic element. Plato's

Of Absolute Government in the Hands of an Individual.

Chapter 8.—We have yet to speak of an absolute government in the hands of an individual; not that it is worthy of much consideration; but in a methodical treatise on the various forms of government, it cannot be passed over. In treating of just and legitimate monarchy, we have pointed out the conditions under which it is expedient for a people, and how it arises. We then mentioned two kinds of tyranny, both of which so far resembled a reasonable monarchy, that they both existed according to established law. The first is, that which is found among certain barbarous nations, who elect an autocrat to rule over them. The second is, that which prevailed of old time in certain states of Greece, the government of the Æsymnetes. These were, indeed, in one respect monarchies, for they were established by law, and received the willing obedience of their subjects. But in another point of view they were tyrannies, for they

---

comment on the Spartan constitution is, that the kingly power, being limited, first by the Senate of 28, and then by the Ephori, was able to maintain itself, and to be the source of safety to others. Ἡ βασιλεία παρ' ὑμῖν, ἐξ ὧν ἔδει, σύμμικτος γενομένη, καὶ μέτρον ἔχουσα, σωθεῖσα αὐτή, σωτηρίας τοῖς ἄλλοις γέγονεν αἰτία. Νόμοι, Lib. iii, c. 11. Edit. Lipsiæ, 1814.

In a passage in the "Politicus" (his ideal of a perfect ruler and Statesman), Plato places in a clearer light what he means by mixed government, namely, "Monarchy limited by good laws;" which, he says, is better than any of the six forms of simple government which he had described, and which are substantially the same as defined by Aristotle; namely, tyranny, unlimited monarchy, oligarchy, aristocracy, democracy, and ochlocracy. Μοναρχία τοίνυν ζευχθεῖσα μὲν ἐν γράμμασιν ἀγαθοῖς, οὓς νόμους λέγομεν, ἀρίστη τῶν ἕξ. Platonis Opera Omnia. Stallbaum. Gothæ, 1841. Πολιτικὸς. P. 297.

ruled despotically, and without consulting any other will than their own. But there is a third form of tyranny, which is most deserving of the name, and which is the direct opposite to a limited monarchy; namely, when one individual, setting himself above the law, rules over his equals and his betters, with no view to the general good, but solely for his own advantage; a government which no free man would willingly submit to.

The Conditions necessary to the best Form of Government.
The best Form of Government is that in which the Middle Classes predominate.

Chapter 9.—Let us now proceed to investigate what is practically the best form of government, under which the generality of men and communities of men, in their ordinary condition, would find their life happiest, and themselves most at ease and contented; for in inquiries of this kind we must look to men in their average state, and not imagine what a community might be if composed of individuals all virtuous beyond the usual standard of humanity, and all endowed with intellectual and moral qualities which require peculiar gifts of nature and no common training. Neither are we going to describe a form of government such as our hopes might picture as most perfect; but a mode of life in which most men in an ordinary state of society might take a part, and a commonwealth not beyond the reach of any community.

Of the aristocracies which we treated of above,

some, such as those presumed to be founded on virtue alone, are above the level of the ordinary condition of man; others resemble so nearly what we have described as a well-ordered commonwealth, that they may be almost included under the definition. Indeed, the solution of all these questions is to be found in principles applicable to all. These principles we have laid down in our Treatise on Ethics, where we have defined a happy life to be one which finds no impediment to the pursuit of virtue; and where we proved that virtue is generally a course of action between two contrary extremes. We therefore come to the conclusion, that the middle course of life is the best, as well as the one most easily accessible to all. Now what is morally true of individuals, is also true of a government; for a government represents the moral life of a community. Accordingly, as in all states there are three great divisions, the very rich, the very poor, and the middle classes, and as it is admitted that a happy mediocrity is the thing most to be desired, it is evident that the best condition of society is that in which the middle classes most abound, for of all classes they are most likely to be governed by calm reason. But the two extremes of society, the very wealthy and the very powerful on the one hand, and on the other the necessitous, the weak, the ignorant, those who neither respect themselves nor others,* are often the most difficult to bring

---

* Σφόδρα ἄτιμον, ... ταπεινοὶ λίαν.

under its control. The first are apt to be contumacious and wilful, the latter wicked; both are disposed to break through the restraints of custom and propriety, and both are often guilty of conduct that is mischievous to the community. Sometimes the one, relying on their wealth, friends, and influence, throw off all obedience; which indeed is of a piece with their bringing up; for even in their earliest years and in their schools, their self-will renders them difficult to control. Those on the contrary who are oppressed with want are generally too submissive; so that a state composed chiefly of these two extremes may be said to consist of tyrants and slaves; the latter unequal to the task of governing, and obliged to submit to arbitrary power; the former resisting control themselves, and ruling the rest despotically. Thence arise envy on the one side, and contempt on the other, and all those enmities which destroy the bonds of political and social life. But the preponderating body in the community should be, as far as possible, one of similar habits, tastes and fortunes. This would chiefly be found among the middle class; and that state will be best conducted which is composed to the greatest extent of those whom we may call its main support and substance. Their position too is the most secure, for they are above committing, and below provoking, injuries and offences. Accordingly thus prayed the poet:—

> "Mine be the middle walk of life,
> More blest, more calm, more free from strife."

It is plain, therefore, that the best commonwealth

is that in which the middle class has the most influence, and is, if not more powerful than both the others combined, yet able, by throwing its weight into one scale, to turn the balance, and prevent either of the others from going into extremes. Wherefore the most happy condition of society is that where the greatest number of persons is found possessing a moderate yet sufficient substance. When this is not the case, but the state is chiefly composed of the extremes of poverty and wealth, that government very soon becomes either an unlimited democracy or an unchecked oligarchy, and soon after that all power will fall into the hands of one man; for a violent democracy and an arbitrary oligarchy naturally give birth to absolutism.

In addition to the reasons already stated, a community in which the middle class predominates is less liable to seditious movements; and in general, in proportion to the extension of that middle class, is the tendency to tranquillity. For the same reason, democracies are usually more durable than oligarchies, for they have a greater number of that class, and these are also admitted to the career of public honours. On the other hand, wherever these are few, and are greatly outnumbered by the lower class, the administration of affairs is ill conducted, and the government soon comes to an end. Solon, Lycurgus, Charondas, and many others who have been most distinguished as lawgivers, have belonged to that middle class.

From what has been already said, we may easily see why the forms of government most commonly found are either democracies or oligarchies; for in general the middle class is not numerous, and in that case one of the two extremes gets the upper hand. Contests, however, are continually arising, and a violent struggle for the mastery is always going on between the wealthy and the lower classes, so that no fair and equitable government is possible, but the chief power in the state is the perpetual point of contention and the reward of victory for one party or the other. Seldom, indeed, have those who founded states been wise or disinterested enough to place the basis of power in the middle classes in the first instance. One man alone, indeed, who was born for power, was induced to establish this political arrangement.* But already the habit had been confirmed in the states of Greece not to look to or wish for this reasonable equality; but some were ambitious to govern, while others were not averse to servitude.

Chapter 10.—In every community the stability of government requires that those who wish for its continuance should be more powerful than those who would destroy it. Now all communities consist of persons and classes of persons differing greatly from each other, and possessing certain broad distinctions that are at once recognised and allowed. This being the case, there are two ways of regarding society for

---

* Solon.

political purposes: one which looks to mere numbers, the other which recognises the different grades and qualities existing among those numbers, namely, birth, wealth, education, refinement, and all the best results of freedom and cultivation. If mere numbers are allowed to have the preponderance, the government will be a democracy; a simple and primitive one, such as the first we described, if the population is solely engaged in cultivating their own lands; but the last and worst form of democracy, if the population is chiefly composed of artizans and day-labourers. If the power of the wealthy and most considerable persons, centered in a few hands, greatly preponderates over that of the many, an oligarchy arises, more or less strict, according to circumstances. It behoves the statesman, therefore, whatever his aims may be, to bind to the institutions of the country the middle classes; for wherever those classes are stronger than both the extremes united, or even than only one of them, the institutions are most likely to be durable; for the wealthy are never likely to combine with the lower classes to overthrow the middle, and thereby to lead to a contest which must end in either the wealthy or the lower classes getting the upper hand without check or control. It is far better that they should seek a middle point between these two extreme results; and if they seek it in good faith and in a moderate spirit (neither of which they are likely to display if acting hostilely to each other), they will find it. An arbitrator is in all cases a thing greatly to be desired, as producing mutual goodwill and confidence. Now, in affairs of state, a middle class is just such an arbitrator; and the more decidedly the institutions are those of a mixed government, the more decisive and effectual will be that arbitration, and the form of government the more lasting. Other political arrangements, which give to the aristocracy an undue share of power, are errors, and sooner or later the imaginary good turns out to be a real evil; for the overreaching ambition of the few is often more destructive to states than the narrow selfishness of the people.

. . . .

Pecuniary Qualification for the Franchise.

Though the needy, and all who are excluded from political power by their poverty or their low condition in society, are generally quiescent, if not ill treated, or deprived by bad government of the lawful means of gaining their livelihood, yet it is desirable to extend, as far as can be with safety, the number of those invested with the franchise.

Formerly, in some of the states of Greece, those only who could bring their own horses into the field, in case of hostilities, were invested with the franchise; and in those times the cavalry was the chief arm in war. They were well disciplined, and accustomed to obedience, for without that an army is useless. But as the population of cities increased, and more men were able to bear arms, the number invested with a share of political power was augmented. The government thence arising they called a democracy; but, inasmuch as in it all orders are represented, we call such an arrangement nowadays, a mixed government. We see, therefore, now, why the ancient states were truly either oligarchical or monarchical; for on account of the smallness of the population they had no middle class. The numbers being few, and all accustomed to discipline, it was natural that they should yield an easy obedience in general matters to those whom they were used to follow.

Of the Deliberative, the Executive, and the Judicial Powers.

Chapters 11 to 13.—Having exhibited the different elements of states, and shown the various forms that they assume, and the reasons of those varieties, we must now explain what is properly called the sovereignty. This complex object resolves itself into three parts, the deliberative, the executive, and the judicial.

. . . . , , . . .

Aristotle here proceeds to define the provinces of these respective powers, and to point out the different modes of constituting them then in practice, by different forms of election or nomination; but as the ancients were confessedly defective in this portion of their political arrangements, and as the great and distinctive merit of our own constitution is the mode in which this difficulty has been solved, by the separation and independence of these leading functions of government, it is unnecessary to follow the author through this portion of his subject. It is sufficient to have indicated the fact of his treating of it, under heads very nearly analogous in substance to those of modern political science.

BOOK V.

Of Revolutions.

Chapter 1.—Since we have disposed of nearly all the other subjects connected with this inquiry, we come at length to that of the revolutions of states, their causes, and the means of preventing them.

It will be found that revolutions arise from the neglect of the great principles of justice and equity; democratic revolutions from the exaggeration of the principle of equality; oligarchical, from carrying to excess the principle of inequality or particular privileges. We have examples of various forms of these revolutions in the different states of Greece.* . . . . A political system of absolute and universal equality is bad; experience proves it to be so, for no government founded on that principle is lasting. The reason is that what is faulty in its origin must of necessity turn out ill. Numbers, therefore, ought to be balanced by wealth and substance, by intelligence and cultivation. Nevertheless, a democracy is quieter and less liable to sedition than an oligarchy, for the latter has two enemies, its own internal factions, and the mass of the people; whereas the people have only one, namely, the small yet powerful body that oppresses them, for their contests with each other are seldom serious. Besides, a democracy is nearer to

---

* The details relate to the particular circumstances of these different states, and are, therefore, now devoid of interest.

the true commonwealth, in which the middle classes preponderate; which is the safest and best of all.

Chapter 2.—Men are tempted to sedition by the love of gain, by the desire of distinction, by the endeavour to escape disgrace or punishment, by envy and jealousy, by an immoderate estimate of themselves; by cupidity, contempt, or other evil passions; by insolence or by fear; or, lastly, to escape injustice or oppression. Sometimes it is a just ambition, as when too many are excluded from the franchises and honours of the state; sometimes it is a lawful fear, which induces men to combine to ward off injustice; sometimes it is a commendable self-esteem, which leads the many to throw off the yoke of an oligarchy, or the few to rid themselves of the disorder and anarchy of a democracy. Thus in Thebes the democracy was destroyed on account of its bad management of public affairs, and in Megara in consequence of the anarchy and confusion introduced by it. The same thing happened at Syracuse until the tyranny of Gelon interposed to stop it; and at Rhodes until it was overthrown by an insurrection.

Changes in political power also arise from the disproportionate increase of some portion of the community. In the natural body, if symmetry is to be preserved, its growth must be uniform in all its parts. So it is of the body politic. In quantity (or numbers), and also in quality, that is, in wealth, virtue, and moral and intellectual culture, its expansion and progress should be harmonious and regular. Yet oftentimes a great and disproportionate development will have taken place in some portion of the community before it has attracted much notice. Sometimes such changes happen all at once, in consequence of some sudden and unexpected event. As an example of the former, the gradual increase of the number of poor in some democracies and commonwealths may be quoted. Of the latter there are many instances. At Tarentum, the numbers of the nobility and the persons of most influence were greatly reduced by the contest with the Iapygians, and afterwards with the Medes. The consequence was, that the mixed commonwealth was superseded by a democracy. The same effect arose from similar causes at Argos and at Athens. When democracies, however, grow wealthy, and the number of men of substance greatly increases, they are apt to change into oligarchies, or even to fall under the absolute government of a still smaller number.

Changes are effected also by faction, or are brought on simply by bad management, or even by the slightest unforeseen circumstances. By the latter I mean circumstances which appear slight at first, and are therefore overlooked, but which are found after a while to have worked a total revolution. This was the case at Ambracia, where the qualification for voting was so small that it was thought that the difference between it and none at all was not worth preserving; but the change produced the most important results.

Great differences of race and dissimilarities of character are also unfavourable to tranquillity. A well-ordered state is not to be formed out of a collection of people suddenly gathered together; and therefore sudden accessions of population have in general led to disturbances and troubles, of which there have been numerous instances in all parts of Greece and Italy, and elsewhere. Differences of locality also have often a considerable effect in engendering feelings of hostility and disunion. At Clazomenæ the inhabitants of the mainland were frequently at variance with those on the island. Instances of the same kind occurred at Colophon and Notium. At Athens the same thing is observable; the inhabitants of the Piræus are much more inclined to democracy than those of the city. For, as in war even the passing over a small watercourse will break the order of the phalanx, so it is in political matters; small causes often lead to great convulsions, no less than the more conspicuous ones of inordinate wealth or great poverty, superior qualifications unduly depressed, or crime unchecked and unreproved. And whenever these small causes of difference arise in regard to matters in which powerful bodies in the state take a deep interest, they should be handled cautiously, and smoothed down, for it has been well said that the beginning is the half of everything, and there is no knowing to what extremities these small beginnings may lead.

The eminent distinction acquired by one portion of

the governing power, or the disproportionate increase of one of its constituent parts, may turn the scale and lead to either an oligarchy, a democracy, or a well-regulated commonwealth. The council of the Areopagus, which gained such credit in the Medean war, appeared to have greatly strengthened the aristocracy at Athens. But the rabble of the Athenian seamen that won the battle of Salamis and the sovereignty of the sea, thenceforth turned the scale of power in favour of the democracy. Again, the Argive nobles, after the battle of Mantinæa, endeavoured to put down the popular government. The popular party of Syracuse, on the other hand, after beating the Athenians, changed their mixed government into a democracy. There are many similar instances; and the struggles usually take place when the extreme parties are nearly balanced, and the middle class is weak or does not exist at all. In that case, the best and most conscientious members of the community take no part in these movements. They are the work of force or fraud, and sometimes of a mixture of both, as at Athens, when she fell under the tyranny of the four hundred.

Of the Causes of Revolution in Democracies.

Chapter 4.—The insolence of demagogues is generally the cause of the ruin of democracies. First, by calumniating the wealthy, they raise these against them, and cause even the most opposite parties to unite against a common danger. Next, they produce the same result by stirring up the populace and creating a sense of insecurity. Many are the examples of this. The democracy of the island of Cos was put down by the persons of property rising against the corruption and wickedness of the demagogues. In the island of Rhodes, the demagogues corrupted the soldiery with the money that ought to have been appropriated to the purposes of the state. The principal people were therefore driven in their own defence to rise and put down the democracy. This form of government was also destroyed at Heraclea by the leading persons of property and influence. These had been expelled by the demagogues, but they returned with reinforcements and extinguished the democracy. A very similar revolution took place at Megara. There the demagogues, in order to gain possession of the public funds and to carry on the government, drove into exile a considerable number of the wealthiest citizens. These at length became so large a body that they returned in force, gave battle to the democratic party, and overthrew it. Precisely the same thing happened at Cumæ; and wherever you turn you find the experience of these changes and revolutions the same. Sometimes they raise the upper and middle classes against them by seizing upon private property or the public revenue, and dividing the proceeds in various forms of bribery and corruption. Sometimes they attack the rich through processes of law, that they may have their property to apply to the support of their government. In former times, when the same men were demagogues in the assembly and leaders in war, the next change was to a tyranny in the hands of one man. Nearly all the tyrants of old began with being demagogues. The reason why it was so then, but is not so now, is, that in ancient times the demagogues led the armies in the field, but were no great orators in time of peace; now, however, since oratory has been so much cultivated, and rhetorical skill so increased, men who are able speakers are the great demagogues, but from want of experience in war they are no longer able to enslave the people, except perhaps occasionally for a short period. Tyrannies also arose in former times oftener than now from entrusting too much power to individual magistrates, as happened at Miletus. For the cities being then small, and the mass of the people living scattered in the country and engaged in husbandry, if their demagogues had enterprise and military skill, they soon got possession of the government.

The great instrument, however, by which they accomplished their ends was, the confidence of the people; and this they won by the hatred they displayed and the persecution they exercised against the rich. Such was the course taken by Pisistratus, when he raised the people of Athens against the inhabitants of the country, and established his power over both. Theagenes did the same at Megara; and Dionysius, by taking advantage of the enmity excited against the wealthy, and impeaching them, enslaved the people of Syracuse.

Changes occur also from the old form of democracy to one still more democratic, in which no qualification is required either for electors or elected. In such cases demagogues, aiming at power through flattery of the people, bring matters to the pass that the populace become masters of the laws and govern as they please. The remedy, or at least the check upon this is, that certain portions of the people should elect the rulers, and not the whole people in mass.

The Causes of Revolution in Oligarchies.

Chapter 5.—There are two most manifest causes of revolution in oligarchies. The first is, the oppression of the people. This they will throw off by the help of the first man they can find to lead them, especially if he happen to belong to the oligarchical body itself, as was Lygdamis of Naxos, who, by the way, afterwards set himself up as the tyrant of his countrymen. The other takes its rise among the upper classes, and occurs when a very few of them have monopolised all the avenues to power, as was the case at Marseilles, at Ister, at Heraclea, and in other cities. There those who were excluded plotted against the government until they brought about a revolution, and obtained admission by turns to all the offices of the state. In Marseilles the oligarchy was thus enlarged. In the city of Ister it was extended to a body of six hundred citizens; but at Heraclea the change ended in a democracy. At Cnidus there was the same cause of contention among the upper classes as at Marseilles; an insurrection took place, and the people, under a leader selected from the better sort, joined the insurgents, who were weak by themselves, and put down the oligarchy. In ancient times, Erythræ also was well and wisely governed by the family of the Basilides; but, not choosing to be governed by a few individuals, the people changed the form of government.

Oligarchies are often kept in a state of disturbance, and finally overthrown, by a species of demagogues belonging to their own class, who excite and mislead the multitude in order to sustain their own faction, as was the case on two occasions at Athens, when Charicles supported the thirty tyrants, and Phrynicus the faction of the four hundred. At other times, the same sort of men have recourse to the arts of seduction and flattery at elections, when the choice of the magistrates or of the judiciary body is in the hands of the people at large, or even of a limited number of them; as happened at Larissa, Abydos, and Heraclea on the Euxine. Sometimes an oligarchy is narrowed into a very small compass, so that those who are excluded are, as it were, compelled to seek the aid of the people in order to regain their position in the government. Men of spendthrift and profligate habits also are a common cause of the ruin of oligarchies, by their attempts to plunder the public, and their quarrels about the division of the spoil; especially if, as at Elis, the ruling body has been contracted to a very small number. But an oligarchy, governing well, and acting harmoniously together, like that of Pharsalus, is not easily overturned.

In time of war, oligarchies have sometimes been overthrown, in consequence of having, through distrust of their own people, called in mercenaries, whose leaders have become their masters, and set up that species of oligarchical despotism called a dynasty. In peace, the cause of the fall of oligarchies has been their various acts of oppression, and arbitrary interference with the rights of individuals.

Changes also happen in the bases of power in oligarchies, and in that judiciously mixed form of government which we have called a polity or mixed commonwealth, by the simple operation of time and of natural causes; as, for instance, when a certain pecuniary qualification has been settled for electors, for the members of the senate, and for the judiciary body, of such an amount as, in oligarchies, to place the governing power in a few, and in commonwealths to place it in the hands of the middle classes; but a long course of prosperity occurring, either in consequence of peace or of some other fortunate events, land and other possessions increase greatly in value, so that the possessions of the poorest come up to the point determined by the census, and give them the requisite qualification. This change sometimes takes place gradually and insensibly, sometimes rapidly and almost at once, and converts the respective governments above mentioned, not so often to their opposites, as to different species of the same form; as from steady and well-regulated governments to unchecked democracies and oligarchies, or from the latter to the former.

The Causes of Revolution in Aristocracies.

Chapter 6.—The causes of revolution in aristocracies are similar to those in oligarchies (for an aristocracy is a sort of oligarchy), and arise from the small number of those who engross power; for if many having equal claims on the score of worth and ability are excluded, an insurrection ensues, as was the case with the Partheniæ in Sparta. Spirited individuals also often disturb the state, if unjustly excluded from power. Aristocracies are also liable to convulsions when the community becomes divided solely into the very rich and the very poor, as has happened after a long course of warfare, by which a country is impoverished, and which causes the people to cry out for an agrarian distribution of property. This happened in Sparta, on account of the war with Messene.

The ambition of a powerful individual to set up a monarchy is also a cause of disturbance in this form of government. But a more frequent one, both in commonwealths and aristocracies, is some error in the original structure; the ingredients of virtue and capacity, wealth, and numbers, not having been well and properly combined. The governments that incline towards oligarchy we call aristocracies, while those that incline rather towards the people are denominated polities or mixed commonwealths. The latter are more permanent than the former, since the majority are masters of the state, and are more disposed to be attached to their government, as it is founded on justice and equity. On the other hand, when power is in the hands of the merely wealthy, it is apt to be misused, and to lead to a selfish policy and to acts of injustice. Generally, a constitution falls on the side to which it naturally inclines; a commonwealth declining to a democracy, and an aristocracy to an oligarchy; but the contrary happens occasionally when a revolution is provoked by the injustice of the upper classes towards the lower, and a sudden and violent change ensues from an aristocracy to a democracy, or from a commonwealth to an oligarchy; for that constitution only is stable which is founded on justice and equity, and which secures to each his own. A change of the above kind happened at Thurium, where a small oligarchy got illegal possession of all the land of the country; the people, who were warlike, rose, massacred the mercenaries of the nobles, and confiscated and divided their estates. Moreover, as all aristocracies partake of the nature of an oligarchy, their tendency is to seek to promote what they conceive to be the interests of the upper classes at the expense of that of the community at large. This was the case in Lacedæmon, and at Locri it caused the ruin of the constitution; measures having been adopted there which would never have been permitted in a democracy, or in a well-combined aristocratical commonwealth.

The alteration of the basis of power in aristocracies generally occurs imperceptibly, and in consequence of the neglect of some little matter which appeared unimportant. We observed above that most constitutions owed their ruin to the neglect at first of some little circumstance; for by overlooking something which touches an essential principle of the commonwealth, they are the more easily led to make some other change, which is somewhat greater than the little one just permitted; and thus by degrees they disturb the whole order and arrangement of the government. An instance of this occurred at Thurium. There was a law that no one should be re-elected to a military command until after an interval of five years. Some young men, distinguished in war, popular with the troops and with the people, and not having much respect for the civil power, set about getting this law altered. The committee of the senate, to whom the matter was referred, were over-persuaded to sanction it, under the idea that the movers in this matter would rest content with this change only, and would not attempt to disturb the other parts of the constitution. Very soon, however, another question arising, they found out that they had lost all their power, that their opposition was fruitless, and that a dynasty, or military tyranny, was set up in the place of their mixed government.

Constitutions are also sometimes overturned by external violence, in consequence of the hostility of powerful neighbours; as by the Athenians and Lacedæmonians in their late contests, and in their endeavours to bring all the states of Greece under forms of government similar to their own.

How Good Governments are preserved.

Chapter 7.—We have now to describe the means by which good governments are preserved; for which we have cleared the way by what we have said of the causes which lead to their destruction. In well-combined and well-balanced commonwealths, besides the strict observance of established laws, it is especially necessary to keep a narrow watch upon little matters. For a great change in the laws may creep on gradually, just as a small expense often incurred ruins a large fortune; and men are apt to be misled by the sophism, that "a mickle is not a muckle." Next, let men be on their guard against those who flatter and mislead the multitude; their actions prove what sort of men they are.

Some aristocracies, and even oligarchies, have been long preserved, not by the unassailable nature of their institutions so much as by the good and wise conduct of the governing body. Dealing fairly and honourably with the interests of those excluded from power, acting in harmony with those of their own class, bringing into office the leaders of the people most distinguished for ability, not repressing the ambitious, not aiming at wealth through the oppression of the poor, they govern with a view to the general good, and avoid those convulsions which arise either from the undue exclusion of men of their own order from power (for aristocracies also have their demagogues), or from allowing power to remain in the same hands too long, and until it becomes impossible to control it.

At times governments are preserved by the very proximity of danger, real or imaginary, just as an officer, in order to keep the night watch attentive, allows them to believe that the enemy is at hand.

Dangerous animosities, especially between the leading persons or most important classes in the community, and political disturbances having for their object a change in the laws, are most especially to be guarded against; and those who still hold themselves aloof from the struggle, should be kept, if possible, from joining in it; and to do this, by discovering and dealing with an evil at its commencement, is not given to any ordinary man, but is the mark of the true statesman. And the census, which regulates the qualification for office, should be revised from time to time, to prevent any undue exclusions, and to obviate the possibility of power being concentrated in too few hands. . . . The even balance of all the different orders of the state should as much as possible be preserved, by strengthening the weak, and increasing the middle class, which is the surest guarantee against the factious designs of either party. . . . We must repeat, that all classes should be well disposed to the existing institutions, so that the number of the discontented should be greatly outweighed by the rest. . . . And it must never be forgotten in a well-balanced state, as it is in those in which one element is allowed to preponderate, that the mean between all these extremes is especially to be aimed at; for it invariably happens, that where one element alone is regarded and becomes paramount, the whole fabric of government is destroyed. Certain deviations from what may be strictly the best, may occur without much injury; as in the human features, a departure from strict regularity does not much interfere with beauty; but in forms of government, an excessive deviation, or disproportionate increase of any one of its constituent points, will first injure and finally subvert the whole. The lawgiver and the statesman should therefore always have their eyes on these principles, and take care that neither party is oppressed by the other. Without both rich and poor, there can be no commonwealth properly so called. If you come to a division of property, you set up some form of government totally different, and, by destroying the existing laws, you destroy the state. A great mistake is made by demagogues in a democracy, when they make war upon wealth, and wrest the laws to their own temporary advantage, and thus divide the community into two hostile bodies; and an equal error and crime is committed by the rulers of an oligarchy, in persecuting and denouncing the humbler classes. Much rather ought their motto to be, "We will do the community no wrong, but govern according to the maxims of justice and equity;" the very reverse of this maxim being the one they generally act upon.

But what will most contribute to the permanence and safety of states, and yet is now much neglected, is an education according to the pattern of the constitution. The best and most venerable laws are of little avail, unless men are brought up to respect them, and to shape their lives and manners in conformity with them. Whatever be the form of government, the conduct to be inculcated should be free from extremes, and should aim at moderation, and to giving effect to the main principle of the constitution, in subordination to, and with the view to promote, the general good. This is often overlooked; in oligarchies, by giving the rein to luxury and effeminacy; in democracies, by carrying to excess the principles of liberty and equality, and by living each for himself and for his own interests. This is bad; for no one ought to think it slavery to live according to a high and good model, but rather to deem it most expedient, safe, and creditable so to do.

Of Revolutions in Monarchies.

Chapter 8.—Monarchies, whether limited or absolute, are liable to the same changes that befall limited governments, and are preserved or destroyed by the same causes. Royalty is a species of aristocracy. Tyranny, on the other hand, is composed of the narrowest kind of oligarchy and of democracy; it is therefore the worst species of rule for the governed, as being the embodiment of two evils, the excess of both the above-mentioned forms of government. Royalty is created by the upper classes of society, to enable them to resist the encroachments of the populace; and originally a king was selected from among the nobles for some personal superiority, or some eminent and distinguished qualities of mind and character. But a tyrant is usually the creation of the populace, in their contests with the upper classes, and as a protection against oligarchical oppression. Nearly all tyrants were originally demagogues, who were trusted by the people to incriminate and attack the nobles. Sometimes they arose out of a stretch of the kingly power by one invested with only a limited authority; sometimes from the conversion of offices of limited duration to offices for life. The kingly power has often been conferred on men of great personal worth, or of highly distinguished descent, or for great benefits effected for the community; as, for the defence of their country in war, or for delivering it from tyranny, or for founding colonies and extending the national conquests, like Codrus, and Cyrus, and the kings of Sparta, Macedon, and others. A king is the national guardian, protecting the property of the rich, and shielding the poor from wrong. A tyrant, on the other hand, looks not to the public interests, but to his own; and while mere selfish indulgence is the end and aim of a tyranny, that of a monarchy is all that is good and honourable. . . .

Injustice, fear, contempt, cause the destruction of tyrannies, as they do of monarchies when they overstep the bounds of lawful authority. . . . They are both also exposed to external violence, from governments opposed to them in principle; and this is very often assisted by domestic discord. . . . The ambition of powerful subjects is a common cause of the fall of tyrannies; and they perish, also, in the hands of successors who become dissolved in luxury, and lose the skill and the courage of their first founders.

Royalty is not easily destroyed by external violence, but, on the contrary, is generally strong enough to put down opposing powers, and is therefore usually an enduring institution. The causes of its overthrow are chiefly these two: the intrigues of its most powerful subjects, and the attempts of the king himself to throw off all control and make himself absolute. These limited monarchies, however, are forms of government very seldom found nowadays, inasmuch as they arise from the voluntary submission of the whole body of the people. The great prevailing equality at present prevents this;* and, moreover, there is no one so raised above the rest as to be equal to the dignity and greatness of the throne, and worthy of a willing homage. We see, therefore, only absolute monarchies, or mere tyrannies, supported by force or fraud. Sometimes limited hereditary monarchies

---

* Aristotle was writing at a time when all the mixed governments of Greece had been destroyed.

fall, through the contemptible character of the reigning sovereign, and sometimes in consequence of his overbearing and tyrannical conduct, which causes the voluntary submission on which his power rests to be withdrawn from him.

How Limited Monarchies are best preserved.

Chapter 9.—Limited monarchies are best preserved by moderation. The more strictly they are limited, the longer they will last. The farther they recede from despotism, and the more they approximate to equality of rights with their subjects, the less are limited monarchs exposed to envy and unpopularity. Hence the Molossian monarchy lasted so long; and hence also the kingly power in Sparta, by the division and limitation of its authority, was increased in real influence and stability. Accordingly, when Theopompus was asked by his queen whether he was not ashamed to transmit to his sons a less authority than he had received from his ancestors, he answered no; for he should transfer to them a throne more steadfast and durable. . . . .

How Tyrannies are maintained.

Tyrannies are maintained by two modes—severity and lenience. The most conspicuous tyrants have been very strict in keeping down all competitors (mowing the tallest stalks, as the saying is), prohibiting clubs and assemblies, putting down meetings for mutual instruction, schools, or other places

of education, keeping men personally ignorant of
each other and unacquainted with each other's movements, and destroying everything tending to generate
mutual confidence and independent spirit. . . . . .
Spies and informers are their principal instruments,
and their great study is, to set man against man,
and class against class. They endeavour, also, to
keep the people poor, in order that, living only from
hand to mouth, they may have neither leisure nor
spirit for revolutions. The Pyramids of Egypt, the
vast building of the Cypselidæ, the Olympian temple
of the sons of Pisistratus, and other great works, are
the records of that kind of policy, and were intended
to employ and to impoverish the people. Inordinate
taxation is also designed for the same end. In five
years the people of Syracuse paid the whole amount
of their property into the exchequer of their tyrant
Dionysius. War, too, is a favourite occupation of a
tyrant, for the sake of occupying the attention of the
people, and making himself necessary to them as their
leader. Those whom he distrusts most are his own
especial friends, as possessing the readiest means of
supplanting him. An unbridled democracy is, in all
its doings, exactly similar to a tyranny. Its objects
and instruments are the worst, and both equally are
served by the tamest and weakest of mankind. A
democracy is always anxious to lord it as a sovereign; it therefore has its flatterers in the shape of
demagogues, and its unscrupulous servants who are
ready for any unworthy action. The leaders of a

democracy must, just like tyrants, have persons to defend their misdeeds, and to please them by flattery; and as no man of a really free spirit, or with a due sense of his own dignity, will condescend to this, such men are hated and feared both by democracies and by a tyrant. . . Such, then, are the wicked expedients for upholding tyranny; namely, the debasement of the people, the destruction of mutual confidence, and the impoverishment of the country, for the better preservation of the tyrant's power. . . .

BOOK VI.
That True Liberty is not found in Democracies.

This book is little more than an amplification of some of the points previously dealt with, and contains little that need be here repeated. Aristotle remarks, that in his time the due admixture of the elements of aristocracy and democracy, in the various governments of Greece, was not sufficiently attended to, and he points to that as the cause of their short duration. He recapitulates the principles on which democratic governments are founded, the chief of which are, "arithmetical equality," or government by mere numbers, without reference to property, or to any especial fitness arising from any considerations, intellectual or moral. The opinion of the majority told by the head becomes therefore law. Thence arises the subjection of the upper classes to the lower, and the consequent licentiousness and tyranny of the latter under the idea that liberty consists in living according to each man's individual will. The laws and usages of democracies, in support of this theory, are then enumerated—the principal of which are, universal suffrage; no property qualification for voting or holding office; the short duration of official power; that no one except military commanders should be elected twice to the same office; that the sovereignty should reside in the assembly, and should be as sparingly as possible imparted to particular magistrates.

Then, inasmuch as birth, wealth, education, with all their intellectual and moral results, are the distinguishing characteristics of oligarchical governments, the opposites of all these have the preference in democracies, namely, low birth, want of substance, want of education and of moral and intellectual training. Under this system no magistracy can be permanent, and if any should by chance have come down from ancient times of any permanent or hereditary character, it must be got rid of, and its power transferred to one appointed by election. These are the properties of democracies. But this "arithmetical equality" is not true equality, nor can true liberty result from it. Without due proportion between wealth and numbers, true equality, and the results to be anticipated from just government, are impossible; and this must be aimed at by the wise admixture of all the constituent elements of a well-ordered state. . . .

Certain democratic governments, of people subsisting on agriculture or pasturage, are next described. These were the most ancient, as well as the most successful instances, of this arrangement of society, and, in Aristotle's opinion, they are suitable only, if at all, to society in that primitive state; but, even in them, he says that the condition of permanence is that there should be a property qualification for magisterial offices, and consequently, the introduction of an aristocratical element; and if the social arrangements are such that the government is, in fact, in the hands of the best and most capable men, and not of men of inferior note or capacity, that may be taken as an instance of the best form of democracy, on account of the good and sensible qualities both of the governing body and of the governed. He adds, that under such a state of society the upper classes, finding themselves invested with a due share of influence, would not be disposed to conspire to effect its overthrow. His maxims of political economy for creating and encouraging the growth of such a community are superseded by those of modern times. Upon the democracies of towns, Aristotle proceeds to pronounce a severe judgment, the ancient stock of the wealthy and substantial citizens in each state having, in his day, been overwhelmed by the admixture of the lowest order of artizans and of foreigners, who had been invested with the franchise through the influence of demagogues. In such, he says, the practice was that

"Ancient customs were to be done away with, ancient ties, civil and sacred, to be broken, everything to be changed according to the new and false theory, in order to level all distinctions, and to enable the multitude to live and to govern according to their will. The result was, an assimilation of democratical to tyrannical government, in its habits and modes of action; for to such a multitude it is far pleasanter to live licentiously, than to submit to the restraints of wisdom and prudence." . . .

Chapter 3.— . . . "The difficulty which those who set up democracies meet with is, not in bringing them about in the first instance, for any one can set up a government of that kind that may last one, two, or three days, but their main difficulty is, in making them permanent. With that view, they should endeavour as far as possible to cut off all sources of pecuniary corruption, to prevent all groundless impeachments, and all proceedings directed especially against the upper classes, and calculated to make them feel that the ruling power is hostile to them.". . .

The mode of doing so, pointed out by Aristotle, has especial reference to the institutions of ancient society, and to the then state of economical knowledge; but he recommends that measures should be taken to cause the prosperity of the people to be permanent, by directing them to employments in which their labour will be reproductive, and, in particular, in sending out colonies to occupy waste lands.

Of Oligarchies.

Chapter 4.— . . . "That species of oligarchy will be most durable which most resembles a well-ordered commonwealth, and which consequently opens freely all inferior offices to the lower ranks of citizens, and associates with itself the best men it can find among the great body of the people. The chief safety is in good government. Healthy bodies, whether natural or political, like sound ships, will bear many hard encounters; but when the body politic, or the natural body, is weak and sickly, it requires tender handling, and, like a crazy vessel, may be knocked to pieces by a slight blow, or wrecked by the smallest mistake of its navigators. As, therefore, a democracy is only preserved by the overwhelming force of numbers, so an oligarchy must look for security from wisdom and moderation."

The other chapters of this book may be passed over. They relate to the details of civil administration, and have little interest except as a record of the civil arrangements in the leading Greek states. The extracts above given from this book have been much abridged, as being little more than amplifications of what had gone before.

BOOK VII.

The Foundation of Public Happiness the same as that of Individuals; namely, a certain Increase of External Prosperity, and the perfecting of our Intellectual and Moral Nature.

Chapters 1 to 6.—Whoever would rightly determine what is the best form of government, must first define what is the best kind of life.

Those people are the happiest (barring unusual accidents), who live under the best government that their circumstances admit.

What, then, is the kind of life most eligible for man in general? And does the well-being of individuals and of communities result from the same causes?

The first of these questions was discussed in the Treatise on Ethics, in which it was proved that the happiness of man depends upon a certain measure of external advantages, on health of body, and on the state and condition of his mind. For no one would call that man happy who possessed neither courage, nor self-command, nor a regard for justice, nor intelligence and good sense. Devoid of the first, he would be liable to be frightened at a fly; without temperance he would wallow in the lowest sensuality; without honesty and a sense of justice, he would, for the sake of the smallest gain, take in his best friend; and in the same manner, if without mental cultivation, he is without judgment, and is liable to be misled like a child; or like one deprived of his reason. A certain portion, therefore, of all these qualities and virtues is, by common consent, necessary to happiness. Most men are contented with their own measure of them; but of estates, money, power, and honour, the desire is usually unbounded. Yet it is indisputable that happiness is the lot of those who lead a virtuous life, and whose minds are most adorned with intellectual cultivation, if possessing at the same time a moderate share of this world's goods; rather than the lot of those who abound in wealth, but are poorly furnished with moral and intellectual excellences. External goods are mere instruments, the excess of which may be injurious or useless; but of mental and moral acquirements and perfections there can be no excess, but the more they abound the more honourable and useful they are to the individual and to society. What comparison can there be between the perfecting the spiritual nature of man, and the acquirement of any amount of external possessions? It is for the sake of the mind only that these latter are worth thinking of, and as far as they contribute to virtue, to wisdom, and to all noble actions. Of this we ought to feel conscious from a consideration of the nature of the Divinity Himself, whose happiness consists not in external objects, but in His own perfections.

External prosperity, therefore, and happiness, are things of a different nature; chance may bestow the one, but not the moral and intellectual qualities which produce the other. And as these qualities are essential to the happiness of an individual, they are no less so for a collection of individuals, gathered together in a well-ordered state. Bad men can never make a good government; for there can be no good action, either from an individual or a state, that is not founded on virtue and wisdom. The courage, justice, and moderation of a government has the same power and form as the courage, justice, temperance, and wisdom of an individual; and it will probably be admitted without further argument, that the virtues of individuals and of governments are the same.

Chapters 7 to 11.—

In the succeeding chapters Aristotle proposes first the question, whether the active or the quiet life be the preferable; and secondly, which is the best form of government? The latter question he answers by repeating his former opinion, that it depends on the circumstances of each individual people; and that "that constitution is the best under which they will be best governed and live most happily."

The former question he goes into at some length, and condemns that political ambition which leads nations to interfere with and to aim at the oppression of each other. He then throws out some considerations respecting the populousness of states, the most convenient extent of territory, the means of offence and defence, national spirit and national character, the influence of climate, and other subjects, his opinions upon which have now no particular interest; but he is led in the course of them to express more clearly and decidedly than he had done before his opinion as to the best form of political society.

The Best Form of Political Society.

He says (Chapter 7): " A community is composed of several essential parts; there must be husbandmen to supply food, there must be arts, arms, wealth, law, and justice; and lastly, though first in importance, due provision for the worship of the Divinity, and priests to serve Him. All these things a well-regulated state requires; for society properly so called is not an unorganized multitude, brought together by chance or accident, but an assemblage of people having among themselves every element of what may be called their life and well-being."

He then recommends a division of labour and a due assignment of employments to individuals according to their different tastes and capacities; and proceeds to say (Chapter 8), that in the state theoretically the best, political power would be lodged in the hands of those only who, by the possession of property, had leisure enough to afford a probability that, by due cultivation of their faculties, they would be found to have ability and character fitting them for the right use of it; carefully and by name excluding those classes who, by reason of their being exclusively occupied with manual labour of the lowest kind, he thought unable to come up to that standard.*

On Municipal Regulations.

Some minute suggestions follow with respect to municipal regulations, and it is especially enjoined that all requisite sanitary measures should be attended to; and in particular that a plentiful supply of wholesome water should be provided; that the streets should be laid out with a view to elegance and comfort as well as utility; and that due care should be taken to place the temples and other public buildings in situations where they would be the greatest ornament to the city.

On National Character.

Chapters 12 and 13.—The next question passed under review relates to the genius and character of the people. Aristotle asks, what is the national character best calculated to promote individual happiness and good government, and how such a disposition may be produced. He says, that the perfection of human happiness requires that we should propose to ourselves the best and highest ends, and choose the best means of attaining them. Nature, custom, and reason contribute towards enabling us to form these dispositions, and to smooth the way for the influence of that education which forms the virtuous citizen, and makes him pliable and obedient to the hand of the wise legislator. In the details of this portion of his subject, however, and in that of education generally, Christian philosophy and modern experience have superseded the views of antiquity. Nevertheless, the high standard of individual, and therefore of national character, which he holds up as the point to be aimed at by the legislator, is worthy of being kept in view.

He says, that his care should be " to consider by what institutions, and by what training, he will be

---

* Aristotle nowhere treats political power as a matter of right, but invariably as a question of expediency, to be determined with reference to the interests of the whole community.

able to form good men, and to develop the best parts of man's nature by directing it to the highest objects. There are two parts of our nature, the higher and the lower. The latter seems to subsist for the sake of the former, and in order, under right direction, to be instrumental to its development. The arts minister to and aid the reason. Labour and business are undertaken for the sake of leisure; war for the sake of peace; the most necessary and useful things for the sake of leading to the most beautiful and the most noble. The legislator, therefore, embracing all these in his consideration, should have regard not alone to the comparatively inferior acts and results, but to those that belong to the higher and better part of our nature, as the ends and objects of our existence. Business and war are right in their turn; but far better are peace and leisure; the things necessary and useful to our daily life are to be attended to; but even more, the true, the beautiful, and the honourable. And to these higher objects should the minds of youth be directed, and not of youth alone, but of all others who need instruction. Great has been the error of some who have passed for able legislators in Greece, in not holding up these highest objects as the aim of their institutions, and in not seeking to develop all the virtues of our nature, but unwisely inclining too much towards the mere useful arts, and those that minister to the desire of gain. Lycurgus has been unreasonably praised for sacrificing everything in his institutions to ideas of war and conquest. Not that the military virtues are not to be cultivated, for without courage and the power of endurance a nation may be exposed to lose its liberties; but they should be regarded chiefly as the means of maintaining peace; and peace and leisure should be made fruitful by the devotion of men's minds to justice and temperance, philosophy and wisdom, in which alone, and not in idle and luxurious enjoyment, consists true happiness."

In the remainder of the present, and in the whole of the last book (the 8th), there is little that is now interesting, the question of education, to which they chiefly relate, being to the ancient world so different in many respects from what it is in modern times. A few sentiments, however, which are put forth in these two books, are of universal applicability, and may very appropriately conclude this abstract of a work which must in all ages excite admiration by its profound wisdom, and by its calm analysis of subjects that most deeply stir the passions, while they most permanently affect the happiness of mankind.

On Education.

Parts of Book 7, c. 15, and Book 8, cc. 2 and 3.—
"In childhood, and in the earliest period of education, have more care for the health of the body than for the mind, and for the moral character rather than for the intellectual. Let nothing base or servile, vulgar or disgraceful, meet the eye or assail the ear of the young; for from words to actions is often but a step. Let nothing of the sort, therefore, be either spoken of by them, or be heard spoken of by others. Let their earliest and first impressions be in all things the best, for we are all governed greatly by first impressions. Let them be taught fully all the essential elements of education, and as much of

what is merely useful in a mechanical point of view, as will not have the effect of rendering the body, the soul, and the intellectual powers, less capable of arriving at the highest excellence of their respective natures; for a too exclusive devotion to some of the mere mechanical arts is apt to injure the bodily faculties, and, by unduly absorbing, to depress the mind. Let, therefore, not those things only be learnt which are the usual instruments of instruction, but those which, like the fine arts, teach us how to enjoy and embellish leisure. The merely useful or absolutely necessary matters of education are not the only ones that ought to be attended to; but to those should be added such as exalt and expand the mind, and convey a sense of what is beautiful and noble. . . . . For to be looking everywhere to the merely useful, is little fitted to form an elevated character or a liberal mind."

POLYBIUS

ON THE ROMAN CONSTITUTION.

(*Extracts from the Preface to Book VI of Polybius's History of Rome. Written about* B.C. 140.)

THE spectacle which the ancient world presented to Aristotle, while composing the treatise with which we have just been occupied, was the prostrate condition of all the governments and people of Greece under the heavy hand of the military power of Macedon, and the expansion of that power to the furthest confines of the East by the genius of the youthful Alexander. Through the calm reasoning and severe analysis of the treatise on "Politics" there gleams a high and patriotic spirit, which seems to aim at recovering his countrymen from the degradation into which they had fallen, by pointing out its causes, and holding up to their view the true models of political wisdom and the pure sources of individual virtue and happiness. But his efforts were in vain, for corruption had too completely enervated the democracy of Athens ; the spirit and form of the admired institutions of Sparta were extinguished ; and the cognate and allied states of the two leading republics were sunk in the same moral and political exhaustion.

A hundred years passed away, and another great power arose from the other side of the horizon. Rome, which in the days of Aristotle and Alexander attracted little notice, had become animated with the vigour which had once inspired the people of Greece, and was proceeding to fill the space in the then civilized world which had been occupied before their day by their illustrious predecessors. Within 130 years after the death of Aristotle, the Roman armies had conquered Hannibal, destroyed Carthage, subdued Spain, dissolved the Achæan League, overrun Asia Minor, and planted their eagles on Mount Taurus, and beside the Euphrates.

Among the principal Achæans sent to Rome as hostages after the final submission of the Greek people, was Polybius, about the year B.C. 167. It appears that, during a residence there of several years, he collected the materials for the history of that people, from the commencement of the brilliant period of their contest with Hannibal (B.C. 220, the beginning of the second Punic war), to the point in their progress which he had himself witnessed. In this design he was assisted by the conqueror of Africa, whose friendship and companionship he enjoyed during many years, being present with Scipio at the destruction of Carthage (B.C. 146), and probably also at the taking of Numantia, B.C. 133.

The first five books of Polybius's history describe the invasion of Italy by Hannibal, and the series of striking events to which that great enterprise gave occasion. The grand spectacle of an untiring national spirit guided by profound wisdom, as exhibited in the firm and finally triumphant resistance to Hannibal, is unfolded with evident admiration and in much detail. The magnanimity and courage with which the Senate and people of Rome had braved the oft-recurring periods of threatening and adverse fortune, impresses his mind as deeply as the great exploits which he had himself seen; which were fast giving them the dominion of the world; and which led them in a few more years to extend their conquering arms from the utmost extremity of Spain on one side to the Euphrates on the other. Struck by these results of the union of resistless bravery with consummate policy, he stops in the course of his history to ask himself, what were the causes that formed a people capable of this greatness? what the form of government "from which, as from a fountain, all these high aspirations, all these daring aims, and all this splendid success had flowed," and which, by its results on the national character, "merited the same praise that you would give to an individual in whom all these qualities of magnanimity and valour were most conspicuous?"*

This question he answers in the Preface to the Sixth Book of his history, and in a manner so remarkable (as a proof that, years after Aristotle wrote, the same principles that had been so elaborately unfolded in the treatise on "Politics" were still recognised as true by the leading minds of the day, and referred to as the guides and standards of political life and true liberty), that, even at the risk of a little repetition in some portion of the following extract, from its similarity to the statements and arguments of Aristotle, it will be acceptable to many readers to see reproduced a large portion of Polybius's remarks on the Roman Constitution, as it affected the development and caused the greatness of that state. He says:—

"That the state of Rome in his day was a matter

---

* Polybius, Bekkeri, Vol. i, p. 495.

by no means easy to be thoroughly understood, on account of the complicated nature of its government; nor could any one comprehend it without a clear insight into all its institutions, public and private. Whoever, therefore, would obtain a precise view of its particular excellences, must bestow on the inquiry much diligent and careful attention."

He therefore follows Aristotle in his enumeration of the three simple forms of government—the kingly, the aristocratic, and the democratic—and in his description of that which is the best of all, namely, that in which all these elements are duly and judiciously mingled, as in Lycurgus's Constitution for Sparta. He then proceeds:—

"As kingly government, and aristocracy properly so called, rest not on force and fear, but on wise laws, just and upright administration, and willing obedience, so popular government is not that in which the multitude is master to do what it proposes and wills, but a government in which it is as it were a household and hereditary custom* to reverence the ordinances of religion, to obey parents, to respect elders, and to submit to the laws. When, under such arrangements as these, the opinion of the majority prevails, we may rightly call such a popular government." . . . .

"There are, therefore, six simple forms of government; the three which were first enumerated, and their three cognate ones—absolute monarchy, oligarchy, and ochlocracy, or government by the mob. First, paternal monarchy arises in a natural manner,

---

* Ὡς πάτριον ἐστί καὶ συνῆθες.

and without art or design. This is followed by monarchy, limited by law and custom. The next change is to an absolute monarchy, or tyranny, which places itself above law. This being intolerable, is put down by a combination of the most powerful, and an aristocracy takes its place. This in turn is naturally succeeded by an oligarchy; but the mass of the people at length rise against the oppression of the few, and establish a democracy; and this again, governing with insolence and disregarding established law, excites hostility, and the measure of change is filled up by the uncontrolled multitude seizing the reins of power. And that this is the true progress of events, may be clearly perceived by any one who will give his attention to consider the sources and the parentage, as it were, of each form of government, and the various changes they undergo; and without this insight into their origins, no one can take a just and comprehensive view of their progressive development, their culminating point, their declension, and their end, so as to be able to point out when and how and under what circumstances the same changes will occur again. More particularly in regard to the Roman government does this mode of investigation seem apt and natural, inasmuch as its origin and progress has corresponded with the order of nature which has been described."* . . . .

In the succeeding four chapters he expands the above brief

---

* Book vi, cc. 3 and 4. (Edit. Schweighauseri.)

sketch of the successive changes to which all the simple forms of government are liable, and which end at length in a corrupted democracy governing by violence and restrained by no sense of justice, "until its uncontrolled and unreasonable will again finds the hand of a tyrant master."*

"This is the circle in which these simple governments revolve, this the natural order in which their revolutions occur, until they come round again to the point from which they set out. Whoever clearly recognises this truth, in speculating upon the future destiny of nations, may perhaps be deceived in the precise time when he anticipates that either of the above changes will come to pass, but he can scarcely be mistaken in his estimate of the particular point at which they have arrived in the course of their development or their decline, or of the next change that awaits them, if he only approach the inquiry without ill feeling or passion. And, as was remarked just above, we shall by this mode of investigation most readily come to a knowledge of the origin, progress, and perfection of the Roman government, and form a right conjecture as to the changes it is destined to undergo; for the course that it has taken from its commencement to the present time is, more than that of any other government, in exact conformity with that natural order of development."†

He then refers to the wise legislation of Lycurgus, by which,

---

* Ἕως ἂν, ἀποτεθηριωμένον, πάλιν εὕρῃ δεσπότην καὶ μόναρχον. (Ch. 9.)

† Chapter 9.

in drawing up the Constitution of Sparta, he sought to meet the defects of all these simple forms of government.

"For, observing these defects, Lycurgus did not set up a simple and uniform mode of government, but brought together, and united in one, all the excellences and peculiarities of each form, in such a manner that no one power, by its disproportionate and undesirable increase, might turn the course of government towards the extreme naturally inherent in it; but each power being held in restraint by the rest, neither should unduly preponderate, to the entire exclusion of the weight and influence of the others; and thus the state, preserving its own weight and even balance, might long endure, and hold on its course like a vessel which, when the wind is strong, is prevented from going to leeward by applying the action of the oars on the leeward side. For the kingly power is restrained from excess by the popular, which has its due share in the government; and, again, the popular power is prevented from encroaching on that of the kings, by their respect for and confidence in the senate, who, being chosen for their public and private virtues and excellences, are always found to throw their weight on the side of right and justice. Accordingly, if any constituent element of the state should happen to be weakened, the elders and the senate, who hold steadfastly by ancient law and custom, throw their whole weight into that scale, and strengthen and support the weaker party. It was by this wise and equitable constitution that

Lycurgus enabled the Lacædemonian people to preserve their liberties longer than any other people with which we are acquainted."* . . .

" The Romans, in forming the constitution of their country, have attained the same end, though not by the same process; for they began with no written constitution like that of Lycurgus, but, after many contests and long experience, and by always taking advantage of circumstances, and choosing the best course, they have framed a constitution which is the very best of all which the world has seen up to the present time." . . . . "For all the three elements above named have their place and influence in their government, but they are so equably and suitably distributed, and the administrative powers of each so well arranged, that no one, even of their own citizens, can pronounce decidedly whether the government should be denominated an aristocratic, a democratic, or a monarchical one. When you look at the power vested in the consuls, you would say it was an entirely monarchical and kingly constitution; when you contemplate the power of the senate, you would call it an aristocracy; and yet if you observe the power that is vested in the people, one would be justified in calling it a democracy."†

He then describes the respective powers and prerogatives of the consuls, the senate, and the people ; but as the distribution of these powers in our own constitution may, without presumption,

---

* Chapter 10.
† Chapter 11. See Arist. " Pol.," Book iv, ch. 7.

be said to be better than any other, and as we have nothing to learn from antiquity on those points, it is sufficient to have exhibited the principle which Polybius so commends, and to have shown that it is in all respects similar to what is in operation among ourselves. He thus terminates his account of the Roman government, which he witnessed in its perfection, and of which he appears unwilling to anticipate the fall :—

"Such, therefore, is the power of each of these divisions of the government for mutual check and mutual co-operation. They are ready to unite to meet every conjuncture, and they thus form a state that is the very best that can anywhere be found. For, when any common external danger compels them to union of mind and will, such and so great is the power of the government, that nothing is omitted that the occasion requires, for all vie with each other in bending the whole vigour of their minds to determine what is best to meet the circumstances in hand. And when this is decided on, no time is lost in delay, but all, whether in their public or private capacity, stretch their energies to carry it forthwith into effect. Therefore is this state invincible, from its very form and constitution; and whatever it determines upon it does. But if, freed from the apprehension of danger from without, and in the full enjoyment of prosperity and abundance—the result of their successes and their victories—they should become luxurious and corrupt, and enter upon a course of insolence and oppression —as may possibly happen—then will the state be seen coming to its own aid, and ministering to its own amendment. For when one of its constituent parts swells beyond its proportionate power, and becomes aggressive, it will immediately be checked by the opposition of the rest, who will suffer no one separate power to get the ascendancy. Everything, therefore, will remain in its place, the impetuosity of some being kept down, and others being deterred from moving, by a knowledge of the opposition they will have to encounter." *

---

* Chapter 18.

EXTRACTS

FROM

CICERO'S TREATISE

ON

A REPUBLIC OR COMMONWEALTH.
(B.C. 54.)

ANOTHER century passed away, from the time when Polybius pronounced the eulogy contained in the preceding pages on the Roman Constitution as it was in his day, and ventured to anticipate for it a long period of existence.[*] He founded his hopes on the self-restoring process which that constitution had undergone on so many occasions in the course of the preceding centuries, and on the fact, which he frequently adverts to in his history, that notwithstanding the great extension of the Roman power and their almost intoxicating successes, "the ancient manners were not yet corrupted," the ancient domestic and social discipline was healthy and strong, and the country abounded in great men capable of serving it with consummate ability and wisdom both in peace and war. Such, indeed, was the height of prosperity and glory to which Rome had risen at that epoch, that the great conqueror of Africa, on becoming invested with the office of Censor, caused the form of public prayer to be changed, and bade his countrymen pray "not that the gods would add to the favours they had bestowed upon his country, but that they would preserve them."[†]

---

[*] Polybius went to Rome B.C. 167. Cicero wrote this treatise B.C. 54.
[†] Valer. Max., Lib. iv, § 10. "Satis" inquit, " bonæ et magnæ sunt (populi Romani res), itaque precor ut eas (Dii immortales) perpetuo incolumes servent."

There were, however, at that very time, seeds of evil in the social and political state, which had begun to show themselves. The aristocracy, by sundry acts of injustice, and by unwise delay in removing just causes of complaint, roused the resentment of large bodies of the people, and gave a legitimate ground of influence to their leaders. The democratic power, gaining the ascendancy, altered the balance of the constitution. The aristocracy, now becoming corrupt with the riches of Asia and the decay of the ancient moral code of Roman manners and discipline, resorted to every means to regain their power. A war of factions was the result, which was withstood and deferred as long as possible by the best and most patriotic citizens, in the early part of Cicero's career, but which he soon very plainly perceived to be imminent, while he foresaw at the same time the downfall of the liberties of Rome and the degradation of the character of his countrymen.

Ten years after his brilliant consulship, in the summer retirement of his villa by the sea-side at Cumæ, he wrote (B.C. 54, and about eleven years before his death) this Treatise on a Republic or Commonwealth, for the sake, as he says himself, of recalling to the minds of his fellow-countrymen the real principles of their constitution, of showing them what it had been in its best state, and how it had arrived at that perfection; of exciting a love and reverence for it in the rising generation; and of endeavouring to bring back the ancient tone of morals and manners "which," he adds, "have so fallen in these days, that the exertions of every good man are demanded to raise them up, to restrain, and amend them."*

With this view he throws his comments upon the true Roman Constitution into the form of a dialogue, supposed to have taken place about a hundred years previously (B.C. 129), between Publius Cornelius Scipio Africanus and a few of his immediate friends and followers, men of the highest position and character in the state, in Scipio's gardens near Rome, during a short remission from public business, at the time of the "Latin Holidays." The very natural way in which these distinguished men seem to be brought together, the frank and affectionate nature of their social intercourse, the grace and dignity of their address, the respect for age and eminent services shown by the younger to the elder—in which even the great Scipio is conspicuous by his manner and language towards his venerable friend Lælius —the beauty of the language, and the truth and wisdom of so many of the sentiments attributed to the different speakers, make this celebrated fragment one of the most interesting and

---

* De Divinatione, Lib. ii, ss. 1, 2.

valuable of Cicero's works.* The treatise opened with a preface consisting of an enumeration of the great deeds of the most illustrious of his countrymen, who in successive ages devoted themselves to the public service, and preferred the labour of political life, its anxieties and contentions, to the ease and tranquillity in which their wealth and station would have enabled them to indulge. The first portion of this preface has not been recovered, but what remains sufficiently indicates the tenour of the whole. It thus proceeds :—

BOOK I.

Chapter 1 (ad finem) to Chapter 8. †

. . . To minds properly constituted, useful and virtuous action is almost a necessity of nature, and the love of contributing to the common welfare is so great, as to overcome all the attractions of a life of sensual and idle indulgence. Philosophers in their studies may define right and wrong, and lay down the principles of morals, but it is the statesman who embodies those principles in laws; who gives the

---

* It was discovered at Rome, in the Library of the Vatican, A.D. 1822, on a "palimpsest," or parchment which had been rubbed a second time to obliterate the first work written upon it ($\pi \acute{a} \lambda \iota \nu$ $\psi a \iota \sigma \tau \grave{o} s$, rubbed over again). This first work was Cicero's treatise "De Republicâ," which, as far as the pages of the parchment itself were complete, was legible beneath the second writing—a portion of St. Augustin's Commentary on the Psalms. It was discovered by Signor Angelo Maio, Librarian of the Vatican, whose edition of it I have followed (Rome and London, 1823), and who shows that, including other fragments of the same work preserved in various authors, we have now about one-third (fortunately the most valuable portion) of the whole.

In giving the substance of this treatise—at least all that may be usefully read at the present day—I have not thought it necessary to adhere to the form of the dialogue, inasmuch as nearly all that gives particular value to the argumentative part of the treatise is attributed to one speaker, Scipio.

† Throughout this "Fragment" several pages in a chapter, and frequently several chapters together, are wanting, but enough has been recovered of the first three books to make up a connected whole.

support of legal sanction to justice, honour, and equity; who sustains public morals, brands what is base, encourages what is noble and of good report, and sets an example of fortitude in peril, and perseverance and endurance in the laborious duties of his high calling. It was said of Xenocrates, a distinguished pupil of Plato, that when someone asked him what advantage his pupils derived from his instruction, he answered, that "they learnt from him to do of their own accord what other men could only be induced to do by the fear of punishment." Few, indeed, are those who thus yield a willing obedience to the precepts of morality and virtue; and therefore great are the services of the statesman who produces a general obedience to them by the compulsion of law, and thus maintains a system of public right, public morals, and a well-ordered government. For my part, as a great and lordly city, as Ennius says, is a grander thing than a little village or a small insulated stronghold, so those who by their counsels and their authority govern the state, are worthy of much higher consideration than those who keep themselves aloof from all public duties; for however great the acquirements of the latter may be, their wisdom, which can hardly coexist with a life of inaction, cannot be of much account. Such men may lead an easy and quiet life, and augment their substance and well-being; and indeed to the pursuit of wealth and to sensual indulgences, mankind are ever too prone to devote their best energies of mind and body; but let us not follow such examples; let us hold that course which has ever been that of the greatest and best of our countrymen, nor give ear to the voice that sounds a retreat, and that would recall from the contest even those who have advanced boldly into it.

To these arguments, so clear and decisive, those who take the other view of the question oppose, first, the labours of public life; as if that was calculated to weigh with a man of active mind and industrious habits; for, to ensure success, what amount of labour is not endured in the humbler professions, in the discharge of private duties, and even in the pursuits of commercial business? They add next, its dangers; using thus the fear of death as an argument to brave men! Which, let me ask, do such men deem most intolerable? to waste and wear away their lives in uselessness and inaction, or to pay to their country a debt which some time or other must be rendered to nature? Again, they think they may safely be eloquent upon the hard measure often dealt out to the most illustrious men, and the injuries they often receive from their ungrateful fellow-citizens; and they quote freely the numerous examples of this in Greek history and in our own, and my own case among the rest, to which they refer with somewhat more affection towards myself and acrimony towards others, because they are pleased to attribute their own and the country's present peace and quietness to my counsels and conduct. As far as I myself am concerned, what happened brought me more honour than labour, more

glory than anxiety; and I felt more pleasure in the
sympathy of the good than pain at the exultation of
the wicked. But had it been otherwise, I should not
have complained, since I had made up my mind to
the worst return from the faction, which I put down
with so much benefit to my country. I knew to what
I was exposing myself, and what sacrifices of personal
ease I was making; for though my own enjoyments
from a life of tranquillity and retirement were greater
than those of most men, in consequence of the ever-
varying delights of literature, in the midst of which
I had lived from my youth upwards, and though my
own share of any public calamity would have been
no greater than that of any of my neighbours, yet
I did not hesitate a moment to stem the torrent of
those evil times, and to meet the storm, for my
country's sake, and at the risk of my own life to procure the safety of others. For I do not hold our
relation to our country, which, like a parent, has
given us life and brought us up, to be this, that she is
to expect no aid and sustenance from us in return,
but only serve to minister to our necessities, to provide us with the conveniences and comforts of life,
and to afford us a sure refuge and a quiet home; I
hold, on the contrary, that she has a strict and irre-
fragable claim that we should devote to her service
all our best energies, our thoughts, our talents and
our counsels, and postpone our private interests to
the duties and sacrifices she may demand of us.

Another excuse which they make to themselves, as

justifying their devotion to a life of mere indulgence, is the annoyance of being mixed up in public life with men of low aims and indifferent characters, and the danger also of such union in times of public excitement. They say that it is not the act of a wise man to assume the reins of government with a knowledge that he may very possibly be unable to curb the unreasonable and impetuous impulses of the multitude; and they ask, whether a man of cultivated mind and manners is to descend into the arena of contest with the unprincipled and the reckless, and encounter misrepresentations and injustice which a prudent man ought not voluntarily to subject himself to. But can there be any stronger motive that ought to weigh with high-minded, virtuous, and brave men, than the determination not to see their country and themselves at the feet of men without principle? For by leaving the course open and unobstructed to these alone, the time would come when the well-disposed, however they might desire it, would find themselves powerless to prevent the most serious evils.

They say, indeed, that when the necessity arises, there is time enough to act. But how, for instance, could I, at the period of my consulship, have acted with effect, had I not gone through all the other offices of the state in regular succession? If you wish to do your country service in a time of danger, the danger must find you in possession of a vantage ground that will enable you to render that service. Neither can I understand the doctrine of men of a certain school, who avow, in quiet times, that they have never given themselves the trouble to learn, neither do they care to know anything of government and of public affairs, but say that they will be ready to take the helm when the storm arises. They allow that they have no special aptitude or knowledge for the work, and that such belongs to men trained and educated in it. How, then, does it become them to volunteer themselves in times of danger, while they admit that even when things are going smoothly, they are unequal to the easy task? Indeed, if it were true, that a wise man ought not to court the trouble of public duties, but at the same time that he ought not to decline them when the necessity arose for his interference, it would, in my opinion, even in that case, be unwise for any man likely so to be called upon, to neglect preparing himself with the knowledge and experience which he may any day have occasion to put to the proof.

Chapter 7.—I have said thus much, because in what follows I am about to treat of a republic, or commonwealth,* which would be of little avail if I had not first endeavoured to remove the hesitation which some have to embark in public affairs at all.

---

* It is almost unnecessary to say that the word Republic, in its modern sense, conveys a very different idea from that intended by the two words "res publica" (from which it is borrowed), in ancient times. In its modern acceptation it scarcely ever implies anything but a democratic republic. Cicero defines it in this treatise (Ch. 25), as "res populi," that is, "the political arrangement which has in view the best interests of all classes and the entire body of the people." The Greeks

If there are any whom I may have failed to convince, I must beg them to listen to those great men, who, like Aristotle and others, though not taking any active part in public matters themselves, yet did in a measure discharge a useful public duty, by their investigations and writings on politics, and to whose authority even the most learned defer with respect. Those seven, indeed, whom the Greeks distinguished above all their countrymen by the name of Wise, were, nearly without exception, men versed practically in political life. And it may be with truth asserted, that in no sphere of action do human powers so nearly approach the divine, as in laying the foundations, or contributing to the stability and welfare, of civil society.

Some who in former times have written on the subject of political government, have themselves had no experience in it; others, though distinguished in active life, have had little skill in literature. The part I have taken in public affairs, during my consulship and on previous occasions, and my early-formed literary habits, give me some qualifications for treating of this subject; nevertheless, what I am about to say lays no claim to the merit of novelty, but is little more than an exposition of the opinions

---

had no similar word; the word Πολιτεία, "Polity," standing as the general term for all governments, which were qualified by the epithets or descriptions appropriate to each, as "Aristocratic," "Oligarchical," "Democratic," or "Mixed," &c.; the latter being, as we have seen, universally held the best, and corresponding to what Cicero calls a "res publica" or "res populi."

of some of the most illustrious men of the best age of our political history.

Chapters 9 to 17.—The different characters of the Dialogue are then introduced, as has been before adverted to, and are represented as meeting during a period of repose from the turmoils of public life, in the gardens of the great general and statesman of the age, P. Cornelius Scipio Africanus. The conversation first turns upon a natural phenomenon which had lately excited attention,—two disks of the sun having been visible at the same time ; and while a regret is expressed at the very limited knowledge of natural science then possessed by those who had made it their study, and the consequent imperfection of their attempts to account for the great phenomena of nature, the utility of mastering such knowledge as existed on the subject is shown by various examples which occurred to men engaged in public life. After an effort at explaining the unusual appearance, so as to bring it within the then existing theory of the laws of motion of the celestial bodies, it is observed :—

How all human things sink in comparison when the mind has been habituated to the contemplation of the works of Providence ; how transitory everything here appears to one who dwells upon the eternal ; how human glory fades before the thought of the small part of the universe filled by the earth itself, and how still smaller in comparison is that portion of it which we inhabit. . . . . How much happier he who sets little store by this world's goods, seeing how small a fragment of them he can really enjoy, and how slight is that enjoyment ; how uncertain also his hold upon them, and how often they fall to the lot of the very worst of men; how much wiser, then, to moderate the desires for all these things, and to be content with what is necessary for daily life ; and to value power and authority, not by the honour and fame it is wont to bring with it, but as opportunities of rendering public service and discharging a public duty. Such a man, having within himself all the best resources for the employment of his time, may say, with some of the best and wisest of our predecessors, that he is never more busy than when he has the full command of leisure, and is never less alone than when alone. . .

Chapters 19 to 22.—Lælius then reminds his friends "that there are other subjects of a nearer interest than that of the cause of the appearance of two suns in the sky at the same moment—namely, the sources of those factions in the state which by their divisions and contests were then almost making two senates and two people out of their formerly united commonwealth. . . . . These natural phenomena are beyond our power, and we know very little about them. But to reunite the senate and the people is a matter within our reach, and if we can affect it, will greatly contribute to the general welfare. . . . . To succeed in this, it is necessary to have studied and to be well acquainted with the principles of government; and to the knowledge of these principles must be added wisdom and firmness in applying them. Let us therefore apply this present leisure to good purpose, and endeavour to induce Scipio to expound to us what he thinks the best form of government, from which we may learn how to establish such among ourselves, and to find our way out of the difficulties that now surround us. . . . . Nor can there be any one better qualified than Scipio for such a discussion, not only on account of his great experience and conspicuous position in the state, but because he has often investigated the subject in former days with Polybius and another learned Greek, whose opinions were, that by far the best form of government was that which our ancestors bequeathed to us, and which was then in vigour."*

Scipio acknowledges that it is a subject to which he has given great attention, and assents to their request.

"For," he says, "when I see the common artizan bending the whole force of his mind upon his calling, in order to attain excellence in it, it would have little become me to show a less diligence in gaining an accurate acquaintance with the duties to which I had been brought up, and which had been as it were left me as a legacy by those who preceded me, namely, the duties belonging to the administration of public affairs. I am, indeed, not quite satisfied with what the most learned of the Greeks have left to us on this subject; nor yet am I quite sure that I can point out anything better. I pray you therefore consider me, in what I am about to say, as still willing to learn; as one who was carefully instructed by my father in all the elements of a liberal education, and fired with a desire of knowledge from my youth upwards, but as nevertheless owing more to domestic precepts and domestic training than to anything I have got from books." . . . .

Chapter 25 to 29.—To proceed, therefore: a commonwealth is a political arrangement which has

---

* See the Extracts from Polybius on the Roman Constitution, p. 78.

in view the welfare of all classes of the community, or, in other words, the whole people. By the word people, I mean not any mere congregation of numbers, but an assemblage of the whole body of the inhabitants submitting to the same laws, and united with a view to the common good. The original cause of their so coming together is not a sense of weakness and the desire of mutual succour, so much as a love of society, which is natural to man. . . . . After thus uniting themselves, they next choose a favourable, that is, a defensible, place for their abode; they then strengthen it by their manual labour, and call this collection of habitations a stronghold or a town, furnish it with temples, and provide it with places of meeting and of public resort. To provide for their security and permanence, they adopt a mode of government which conforms to that of their origin; either one man alone being placed at their head, or a certain few chosen from the rest, or a government is constructed formed from the mass of the people. The first is called a simple monarchy; the second an aristocracy; and the third a popular government, or one in which the chief power resides in numbers. Either of these is tolerable, and one may under particular circumstances be preferable to the other, provided all promote the common good, and therefore fulfil the original object which united men together in society; but I consider neither of those forms perfect, or worthy of being called the best. An absolute monarch may be wise and just; so also may be the government of a few; and even that of mere numbers, though the least desirable of the three, may possibly be stable and firm, and be neither allured by cupidity nor hurried away by passion. But in an absolute monarchy, the subjects are unjustly deprived of their common rights, and of the power of deliberating for the common good; under the domination of an aristocracy, the many have little security for their liberties, since they are not consulted and have little power; and, lastly, where all power is in the hands of the many, though they may use their power justly or with moderation, yet the very equality is unequal and unjust, since it admits of no gradations of rank and dignity. Accordingly, I should not like to have lived even under that most just of monarchs, Cyrus, inasmuch as the government and the common welfare depended solely on his will. Neither is the government of our friends, the aristocracy of Marseilles, to be approved of,* for under such a constitution there is too great a resemblance to a state of servitude, in the relation of the lower classes to the upper. Nor can we commend the Athenians for destroying the council of the Areopagus, and carrying on the government solely by popular decrees, for in so doing they abolished all ranks and dignities, and deprived the state of its best ornaments. And these objections which I have

---

* Aristotle refers to the government of Marseilles, in Book v, ch. 17, of the "Politics."

stated, apply to such governments even in their best state, before corruption has taken hold of them and produced the confusion which follows from it. But all these simple forms have, in addition to the objections just adverted to, other faults, or rather, pernicious vices, into which they are prone to fall. For an amiable monarch like Cyrus, whose government may be light and easy, may be converted by some fickleness of mind into such a tyrant as Phalaris; since the unrestrained power of one man slides by a very gentle and imperceptible transition into a tyranny such as his. Again, the aristocratic power wielded by the few at Marseilles is not far removed from the mode of administration adopted at Athens by the faction of the Thirty Tyrants. And at Athens, the unrestricted power of the people soon degenerated into the rage and license of the mob. . . . .

But these simple forms are seldom lasting,

" giving place in turn, the one to the other, as circumstances and occasions may favour their growth and predominance. And strange, indeed, are the courses of revolution in these governments, and various the orbits, as it were, in which they move. It is the statesman's business to be acquainted with these changes and their causes, and to prognosticate their approach. And if he takes his measures accordingly, and succeeds in keeping the direction of them in his own hands, he displays one of the greatest efforts of human wisdom."

Such being the imperfections of these simple forms, and their liability to constant change,

"there remains that last species of government which is the best of all, namely, that which is moderated in its action and steadied in its course by the due admixture of all the three simple forms of monarchy, aristocracy, and popular power." . .

Chapters 31, 32.—Liberty can have no certain dwelling in any state except where the laws are equal, and the power of public opinion supreme. . . . . Where the whole community is in possession of their just rights, a condition of society exists than which nothing can be happier, greater, or more free. This alone can with propriety be called a commonwealth, when the interests of the whole people are connected, and the government is conducted with the sole view of promoting the common good. Accordingly, the domination of an absolute monarch or of an aristocracy gives place at last to that; while, on the contrary, a free people are never found to make a voluntary surrender of their rights to either of the former. Nor should a state of freedom be feared on account of the evils that arise from its excesses, when an unbridled democracy may happen to get the upper hand. If the whole body of the community act together, and have no other object in view but the common welfare and the preservation of their common liberties, no such excesses can arise, nor can the firm and equable action of such a government be easily impeded or disturbed. Concord and harmony naturally prevail under that state of things, inasmuch as everything works together so as to promote the interests of all; whereas where interests clash, and what seems desirable for one portion of the community is injurious to another, the result can be no other than ill-feeling and discord. Thus, under the ancient aristocracies, which legislated for their own narrow interests alone, the position of the government was never stable. Still less was it so under the absolute monarchies to which, as Ennius said, their subjects were never bound by the ties of honourable and conscientious allegiance. Law is the bond of civil society, and equality in the eye of the law the right of every citizen. You do not choose to attempt to equalize wealth, and it is equally impossible to equalize the talents and genius of mankind; the laws, however, you can make just and equal for all those who live under them. . . .

Chapters 33, 34.—A free people will exercise its choice in regard to those to whose government it will entrust itself; on the discretion it shows in exercising that choice, its very safety depends; it will choose, if it is wise, the very best men it can find; for the united counsels of such are often not less than are essential to the public welfare. Nature herself points out that it must be so, by fitting for command those gifted with superior intellectual and moral powers, and by disposing the weaker to obedience. But this excellent and natural state of things is very apt to be overthrown, when the opinions of the unenlightened and the bad obtain the ascendancy. Such men have nothing in their own minds which enables them to judge of those high qualities in others.

Accordingly the more wealthy, who in the earlier stages of society were also the noble, were, if they resorted to corruption, selected for the offices of government. And to such a mode of government they persisted in giving the name of aristocracy, or the rule of the best men, although it little deserved the appellation, inasmuch as, by the error of the people, mere wealth was placed at the head of the affairs, and not virtue and ability. Indeed, wealth, titles, and power are sources of disgrace rather than of honour, and the parents of pride and insolence, when their possessors dispense with the lessons of wisdom, throw off the habit of self-command, and use no measure or consideration in their mode of governing others. There can scarcely be a more repulsive state of society than that in which wealth alone is considered the standard of excellence. But when men of virtue govern the state; when he who commands others is himself enslaved by no base desires; when he is an example of that cultivation and refinement to which he would lead and train his fellow citizens; when he imposes no laws on others which he does not himself obey, and exhibits in his own life a rule and pattern for his countrymen;—when such men govern a country, what can more conduce to its honour and renown? If one such man could embrace all the functions of government, there would be no need of others; and if all men could see what would be the best course to take in political affairs, and unite in taking it, no one would feel the want of men chosen for the special purpose of advising: but the difficulty of coming to right conclusions on important subjects has from time to time caused the transference of authority from one man invested with large powers to a council or assembly; while, on the other hand, the mistakes and the rashness of popular governments have occasioned the concentration in a few hands of power that had for a time been exercised by the people at large. Between these extremes, between the infirmity of one individual and the rashness of many, an aristocracy holds a middle place. Its characteristic, when in its best state, is moderation; and when a government of this kind presides over public affairs, the people at large are happy and free from anxiety; those who are entrusted with their interests devote themselves to the task, and take care that the people never have cause to complain that they are neglected. Under this system of government, honours and dignities, of different degrees of estimation and value, must necessarily exist, as they do, indeed, even under those governments where the popular power is most unrestrained and absolute; for even among these there is a great ambition for places of dignity, and a great competition among candidates for them; for the rigid equality which some free countries favour in theory cannot be preserved, or, if it is, it produces the greatest injustice. According to that theory, the highest are confounded with the lowest and most abandoned, and such there will be under every government; and the pretended equity becomes most unfair and unequal. Nothing of this kind can happen under the moderate aristocracy which has been above adverted to. . . .

Chapter 35.— . . . You are right in asking which of these three forms I most approve of, for I entirely approve of neither of them, when by itself and separated from the others, but greatly prefer, and consider better than either, a form of government that is composed as it were by the fusion and combination of all the three.

Chapters 36 to 39.— . . . By the common consent of the world, political society took its origin under the kingly form of government. It was so with the people of Rome. But after a time, they conceived a hatred for the very name of a king, in consequence of the haughty tyranny of Tarquinius; they drove him into banishment, and, in the exultation of their newly-awakened energies, rushed at once into unbridled license. Under this excitement they banished many innocent men, and confiscated their property; they appointed the consuls for one year only; they claimed the marks of honour hitherto given to their kings; they caused all public questions to be submitted to their judgment; they broke out into rebellion, and finally engrossed all the powers of the state. . . . . This continued as long as peace and tranquillity lasted, but amidst war and dangers they submitted implicitly to their magistrates, since they regarded their safety more than the satisfaction of their passions. Indeed, when perils were imminent, they have been wont to place the whole power of the state in the hands of a single individual, whom they named a dictator; sufficiently indicating by the very name the absolute nature of his authority. . . . .

Chapters 41 to 44.—Our ancestors had a great reverence for the kingly power; they were accustomed to call their kings, not their lords and masters, but the guardians of their country, and they regarded them as the source of power and even of their political existence; and that disposition would have remained in the people if kings had ruled justly. The tyranny of Tarquinius gave a death-blow to that constitution among ourselves. . . . . And, indeed, in every political society in its early stage, the change from this mode of government to another is inevitable. An unjust king arises, and is put down; another succeeds, worse than he, and becomes a tyrant, and he in turn is generally mastered by the upper classes. These unite and form the second species of government which has been mentioned, namely, an aristocracy, which partakes somewhat of the kingly power; for such or somewhat similar are the qualities of an aristocratic assembly that directs its measures with a view to the general good. If it is the popular power that rises and overthrows a tyranny—in that case, the use they will make of their victory, the stability of the government they will set up, the moderation they will show in the midst of their triumph, will depend on the progress they have made in wisdom and discretion. But if the popular violence declares itself against a king who has given no good ground of offence; or if, as more frequently happens, it attacks aristocratic power, commits excesses, sheds blood, and prostrates every power of the state before its cupidity and passions, you may as well undertake to quell a raging sea, or to extinguish a vast conflagration, as to restrain such a multitude, insolent with success, and heedless of all control. Then that state of things arises which has been so admirably described by Plato in his book on a republic. "For when," he says, "a city has fallen under the hands of demagogues, then the people, athirst for more and more liberty, become intoxicated with its immoderate draughts, demanding it from servile ministers, and insisting upon having it, not tempered, but unmixed and pure. Then they turn upon their magistrates, and if they do not find them yielding and subservient, and ready to submit to all their demands, they accuse and punish them as oligarchs and tyrants. Those who obey the magistrates they abuse and despise; on the other hand, the men who, though invested with power, submit to dictation, or who, though filling only a private station, assume the attributes of power, they extol with praises and overwhelm with flattery. Such a city, indeed, will have its fill of liberty, which will penetrate into every family, and end in establishing anarchy throughout the whole range of domestic life. For it will grow into a habit to place the father on a level with the son, which will breed between them mutual suspicion and fear. There will be neither respect nor reverence for parents, lest, forsooth, it interfere with one's liberty.* You will be taught that your neighbour is not more to you than a stranger, and that the latter is to be considered on an equal footing with the former. In such a state of society, the teacher fears and flatters his scholars, and the scholars despise their pastors and masters. The young put themselves upon an equality with the old, contend with them in argument, and ape their actions; the advanced in years descend to the level of the young, imitate their doings, and take the lead from them in manners and conversation, lest they should lose their favour and appear despotic. Servants and masters, wives and husbands, are upon the same degree of equality; and, as the proverb says of wild horses and other ungovernable animals, you must get out of their way unless you wish to be run over. In all the other relations of life the same unlimited liberty prevails; and the result of it all is, that such a people are first indignant at the slightest species of control, and then end by throwing off respect for the authority of all law, written or unwritten, lest it should be thought that they have in

---

* Οἷον, ἔφην, πατέρα μὲν ἐθίζεσθαι παιδὶ ὅμοιον γίγνεσθαι καὶ φοβεῖσθαι τοὺς υἱεῖς, υἱὸν δὲ πατρί, καὶ μὴ τε αἰσχύνεσθαι μὴ τε δεδιέναι τοὺς γονέας, ἵνα δὴ ἐλεύθερος ᾖ . . . . καὶ ὅλως οἱ μὲν νέοι πρεσβυτέροις ἀπεικάζονται καὶ διαμιλλῶνται καὶ ἐν λόγοις καὶ ἐν ἐργοῖς.—Πολιτεία H. Edit. Bekker. Lond. 1825, p. 442.

A similar passage in Plato's Book on "Laws" traces the decline of morals in his time from disobedience to parents, and want of reverence to superiors, to the abandonment of all respect for law, honour, or religion. . . . . νόμων ζητεῖν μὴ ὑπηκόους εἶναι, . . . ὅρκων, καὶ πίστεων, καὶ τὸ παράπαν θεῶν.—Νόμοι, Lib. iii, ch. 16. Lipsiæ, 1814.

any way a master. . . . From this license, tyranny springs as certainly as a tree from its root. As an oligarchy perishes from the possession of too great and unlimited power, so a too free people are reduced to slavery by the very excess of liberty. In reality, excess in anything is wont to lead to its contrary; as we see in the seasons, in the premature growth of plants, in the conditions of health in the human body. It is not less so in matters of government, for excess of liberty is accustomed to give place to nothing else than to excessive slavery, whether in the case of an individual or a state; from no other institution, therefore, than a democracy, is tyranny more likely to spring; and the more licentious the preceding state of freedom, the more complete and severe will be the servitude. They usually choose some active agitator who has distinguished himself by his attacks on the wealthy, and, placing him at their head, support him in power until he acquires real influence. This he effects in the common way, by surrounding himself with guards, as if for the protection of his person. At length he plays the tyrant over the very men who set him up. The change may be for good, as often happens when a good ruler puts down a tyrannical faction. But it may be the contrary. Thus, under these simple forms of government, the state is liable to be bandied about, as a ball, from one to the other, and to find stability and repose in none of them." *

---

* I have translated this passage from the original, instead of from Cicero's version of it.

Chapters 45 to 47.—Of the three first and simple forms of government, the monarchical is in my judgment the best—.

That is, in the words of Plato, the monarchical defined and strengthened by good laws.

But this species of monarchy is itself excelled by the government which is tempered and balanced by the due admixture of the three best forms above described.* For it is desirable that there should be in the state some element that is pre-eminent and regal;† another that has been won by, and is willingly yielded to, the weight and dignity of the aristocracy;‡ a third consisting of matters reserved for the judgment and the will of the people at large. This constitution has in its favour, first, a certain great and conspicuous principle of equity, § which free men will not long consent to be without; next, firmness and stability, which distinguishes it from those first-mentioned simple forms that run so readily into their contraries, a monarchy becoming a tyranny, an aristocracy a faction, a democracy mob-government and confusion; each vicious excess often giving birth to some new form of tyranny. These changes cannot happen where the framework of government consists

---

* Regio autem ipsi præstabit id quod erit æquatum et temperatum ex tribus optimis rerum publicarum modis.
† Quiddam præstans et regale.
‡ Aliud auctoritate principum partum ac tributum.
§ "Hæc constitutio primùm habet æquabilitatem quandam magnam," not "equality," but "equity," "consistency" with itself and with the order of nature."

of the discreet union of the several powers, as above defined, unless through some great errors and vices of the leading classes of society. For no legitimate cause of change exists when each man stands firmly on his own ground, and no pitfall is near into which he could be precipitated.* . . . .

"It is my fixed and firm opinion," adds Scipio, "that no form of government was ever comparable, either in its limitations or its discipline, to the one which our fathers received from their predecessors and transmitted to us. Although, as you rightly say, it has been altered by the late seditions,† I will, nevertheless, expound to you its principles, and exhibit to you, since you desire to hear my views upon it, its many excellences."

The remaining part of this Book has not been recovered.

BOOK II.

Chapter 1.—Seeing then the minds of all his audience fixed in earnest attention, Scipio thus proceeded :—

"The opinions I am about to express are those of

---

* The often-quoted opinion of Tacitus, "that the mixed form of government is easier praised than discovered, or, if brought into action, would probably not be durable" ("delecta ex his et consociata Reipublicæ forma, laudari facilius quam evenire, vel, si evenit, haud diuturna esse potest."—Tac. Ann., Lib. iv, § 33), must be considered in reference to the context, which is a lamentation over the degradation of the public manners, and the consequent extinction of Roman freedom. "Nobis . . . . inglorius labor . . . . Nos sæva jussa, continuas accusationes, fallaces amicitias, perniciem innocentium, et easdem exitu causas conjungimus; obviâ rerum similitudine, et satietate."

The great cause of the ruin of freedom, pointed out by Cicero in the passage in the text—the corruption of the upper classes—(magna principum vitia) had been fully realized in the time of Tacitus.

† Lælius, "etsi ne nunc quidem."

the venerable Cato, to whom, as you know, I was attached by the strictest bonds of friendship, whose character won my greatest admiration, and to whose society the advice of both my parents and my own good-will led me to dedicate myself from my youth upwards. Of such intercourse it was impossible to tire, so great had been his experience of public affairs, which he had conducted for many years with the greatest success both in peace and war, so great was his moderation in speaking of his own actions, and so well did he know how to mingle pleasantry with dignity. His conversation was, as it were, a picture of his life; and, withal, he was not more willing to teach than ever desirous to learn. On the subject of our constitution he was accustomed to say that there was one especial reason why it was superior to all others. In nearly all other countries it had been some particular individual who had framed the government on the model of laws and institutions drawn up by himself. Thus the Cretans received their laws from Minos, the Lacedæmonians from Lycurgus; and the Constitution of Athens, which has undergone so many changes, was first framed by Theseus, then modified by Draco, next by Solon, next by Cleisthenes, and after him by several others; finally, the well-nigh lifeless and prostrate body politic has been taken in hand and supported by Demetrius, a professor. Our constitution, on the other hand, is not the result of one man's genius, but of many; neither did it come into existence in one man's life, but has been built up in the course of centuries, and by the efforts of many generations.* He used to remark, that no individual genius ever did, or probably ever would exist, who, in framing a form of government, could provide for every contingency. He thought that not even the collective ability of a whole people, at any one particular period, was equal to the task of foreseeing all that ought to be comprehended in their scheme; a result only to be expected from time and experience. Wherefore we must go back, as was his wont, to the origin of our political state; and if I show you our constitution in its commencement, in its progress, and in its firm and vigorous maturity, I shall better expound its principles, than by exhibiting it in comparison with any imaginary standard, such as Plato's version of an ideal republic." †

An eloquent and interesting sketch follows from Chapter 2 to Chapter 22 of the origin of the city of Rome, its favourable position for commerce and defence, the commencement of its elective senate, its religious institutions, its penal system, the early struggles between the aristocratic and popular power, their difficulties in adjusting the balance of authority between themselves and the executive, and the encouragements given to agriculture and the arts of peace, as well as to those of war. An outline is then given of the character of the successive kings, and of the steps made towards perfecting the constitution, and providing for the public health and recreation. In particular, that change in the mode of voting in the elections for the

---

* The editor, Signor Maio, adds in a note to this passage, "The English political writers speak of their constitution in almost these very words" (sic fere Britanni politici de suâ republicâ loquuntur).

† This imaginary scheme of civil polity he afterwards (Ch. 11) designates as "having nothing akin to real life, and abhorrent to men's habits and morals." Its doctrines have nevertheless been revived, as the foundation of modern Communism.

senate is remarked, by which the influence of property was increased, in comparison with that of mere numbers, "and care was taken, as always must be in a free government, that mere numbers should not have a preponderating power" (curavitque, quod semper in republicâ tenendum est, ne plurimum valeant plurimi). (Chapter 22.) "By voting, not individually, but by classes and centuries," the invidiousness of exclusion was avoided, and at the same time, also, the danger of the predominance of mere numbers. The names, too, of the different classes were significant of their social position; as, for instance, those who contributed the smallest amount of taxes were called "proletarians," as giving little more to the state than the increase of population in their own offspring.° Also of the whole ninety-six "centuries" a greater number were combined to make up one vote than the whole first class consisted of. Accordingly, every one had a right to vote, but the preponderating influence was preserved to those who had the greatest interest in maintaining the country in its best and highest condition." (Chapter 22.)

. . . . Chapter 23.—"This three-fold combination of powers above described is common to us and to other governments. But what we have attained to, as our peculiar distinction, is, the manner in which these several powers are tempered and brought to act in harmony. This was not so in Carthage or in Sparta, where the regal power had too great a preponderance. Such a government is ever liable to change, as depending too much on the vices or virtues of an individual. Yet perhaps the regal form is better than either of the other simple ones, as long, at least, as it preserves in purity its own theory, which is, the embodiment of justice and wisdom in one head of the state, and the good treatment, the safety, and the tranquillity of the governed. But to a people

---

* Proletarios nominavit; ut et iis quasi proles, id est, quasi progenies civitatis expectari videretur. (Ch. 22.)

under a government of this kind, many things are wanting, and in the first place, liberty; for this consists, not in our having a just master, but in our having none."

Chapter 24.—Instances are then given of this mode of government and its results, generally ending in "Tyranny," a brief and very dark picture of which is given, and which is described as incompatible with the smallest amount of liberty (Chapter 27). From this point the manuscript becomes so fragmentary that the thread of the argument is entirely broken. From what remains, however, it appears that it relates to the various laws passed from time to time, which contributed, each within its own sphere, to make up the whole fabric of the Roman Constitution and social state. It attained perfection, according to the opinion attributed to Scipio, when—

Chapters 32 to 34.—"The senate possessed the principal weight in the government. Though the people were free, their direct action was less than that of the senate, who, supported by law and custom and by their own weight and dignity, had the chief share in the administration of public affairs. The consuls, indeed, held their office for one year only, but their power was in fact regal. The votes of the assemblies of the people were of no avail unless ratified by the senate; an arrangement which preserved the authority of the latter, and which they defended with great determination. Only ten years elapsed from the first creation of consuls, when, in a period of difficulty, a dictator was appointed, with apparently uncontrolled regal power. Yet all the branches of administration continued to be carried on with undiminished authority, by the leading persons in the state, the popular power being for the time suspended; and great and noble actions were in those days performed by men of the highest distinction, invested with great commands, both in peace and war.

"A few years only passed on, and the people, as was natural after the attainment of their first liberties, gained a little more power; more perhaps than the occasion required; but it is the nature of public affairs often to bear down reason. Remember, however, what I said in the beginning of this discourse—that unless there is an equitable adjustment in a state, of rights, offices, and functions, so that the executive may have sufficient power, the senate sufficient authority, and the people sufficient liberty, the frame of government cannot remain stable and free from violent change. This consideration was overlooked in the early days of our constitution, and led to popular outbreaks, as it had before in Sparta and in Crete, and to the diminution of the power and authority of the senate. Nevertheless, in spite of these circumstances, the senate sustained itself in great power and dignity, supplying as it did to all the offices of administration men of great wisdom, great bravery, and consummate prudence. They continued, therefore, to stand very high in the public estimation, not only on account of their honour and renown, but of their private virtues, —their self-command, their comparative strictness of life, and their liberal and generous expenditure. Their public virtues were invested with a greater grace because in their private conduct they exerted themselves with the greatest diligence to aid, to counsel, and to defend their fellow-citizens."

The progress of decline in the Roman institutions is then touched upon; but so much of this and the remaining part of the work is lost, that no good purpose would be answered by pursuing it further. Enough, however, has been given to show that the object of Cicero in this Treatise was, to warn his countrymen against the corruption which was visibly in progress in his day, and to remind them that their liberties could only be maintained by adhering to the principles of public conduct and private virtue that had distinguished their forefathers. " Tamen de posteris nostris et de illâ immortalitate rei publicæ sollicitor; quæ poterat esse perpetua, si patriis viveretur institutis et moribus."—Book iii, fragment of Chapter 28.

[The following remarks of John Stuart Mill on the peculiar value in the present age of such thoughts and reasonings as have occupied the preceding pages, may be not unacceptable in this place:—

"De Tocqueville was right in the great importance he attached to the study of Greek and Roman literature; not as being without faults, but as having the contrary faults to those of our own day. Not only do these literatures furnish examples of high finish and perfection of workmanship, to correct the slovenly habit of modern hasty writing, but they exhibit, in the military and agricultural commonwealths of antiquity, precisely that order of virtues in which a commercial society is apt to be deficient; and they altogether show human nature on a grander scale; with less benevolence but more patriotism; less sentiment but more self-control; if a lower average of virtue, more striking individual examples of it; fewer small goodnesses but more greatness, and appreciation of greatness; more which tends to exalt the imagination and inspire high conceptions of the capabilities of human nature. If, as every one may see, the want of affinity of these studies to the modern mind is gradually lowering them in popular estimation, this is but a confirmation of the need of them, and renders it more incumbent upon those who have the power, to do their utmost towards preventing their decline."] (Mill's Dissertations, Vol. ii, pp. 68, 69.)

PART II.

INTRODUCTION.

[DURING the many centuries of the decay of the Roman Empire and the almost entire extinction of liberty, no opportunities were afforded for the philosophical discussion of the principles of government. When freedom had again revived in the Italian republics, and while these, after periods of prosperity, were running the same career as their predecessors in ancient times—of disturbances, convulsions, extreme counsels, ambition, war, exhaustion, and finally loss of liberty and subjection to military power —the study of the principles of politics attracted a few leading minds,* among whom were Dante (1265— 1321) and Petrarch (1304—1374), but neither treated the subject fully. In his Dissertation on Monarchy, Dante, from his experience of the troubled times in which he lived, was led to the conclusion that the peace of the world and the elevation and happiness of society could only be secured under a monarchy. He says, that "he reads in the history of the Past,

---

* Blakey's History of Political Literature from the Earliest Times. London, 1855. Vol. i, p. 472.

and it pains him to witness in his own day the storms, the injuries, and the destructions which the many-headed factions that alternately bore sway had inflicted upon his country." Petrarch's great aspiration was to re-establish the seat of the Western Empire in Rome, as a refuge from civil strife. In his three political "Canzoni" (the 3rd, 6th, and 16th), and especially in the one addressed to Rienzi, he mourns over his country, exhausted by long civil feuds, and endeavours to rouse his fellow-countrymen against the foreigner; a desire only fulfilled after five more centuries of oppression.

It was not until the early part of the 16th century that the systematic study of politics revived for the first time since Cicero's Treatise.]

MACHIAVELLI.

(1469—1527.)

The conspicuous place occupied among his contemporaries by the statesman and historian, Machiavelli, qualified him for the task he undertook, of interpreting the political history of Rome to his countrymen.

In the Dedication and in the Preface to his Discourses on Livy (written about the year 1513), he mentions his motives in writing them. He refers to his own studies in ancient literature, and to his long conversance with public affairs; to the neglect into which the study of the Past had fallen, and the consequent want of the political lessons that are largely taught by it. "So little is now generally known of the great examples which the history of their own country affords, and the instruction to be drawn from them, that scarcely a sign remains of the antique virtue which made its former power and fame."

In his Discourses,* or commentaries on Roman history, he is ever keeping in view the instability of the governments that had been so long the bane of his own age; the frequent changes from a tyranny to a democracy, and from a democracy to an aristocracy. He holds up to his countrymen their own picture. He describes the changes that the Roman people had passed through in all the stages of their history, and their causes; and he puts before them the experience, the truths, and the maxims that had been the guides of the statesmen of ancient times.

After describing the different kinds of government— that of a monarchy, an aristocracy, and a democracy,— and the steps by which they are liable to give place the one to the other—he says, that the wisest and best form, and that which is most firm and stable, is one in which the powers of the three are blended together. He instances the Constitution of Lycurgus for Sparta, and the government of Rome under the tribunes. "In these, the legislator did not take away all the qualities of the regal power to give it to the aristocracy,

---

* I Discorsi di Nicolò Machiavelli. Parigi, 1825.

nor did he diminish the authority of the aristocracy to give it entire to the popular branch; but the constitution of the state being mixed became perfect."

Machiavelli notices how important a part Religion played in forming the character of the Roman people in their best period, and causing their greatness; how essential prudence and circumspection are in introducing reforms; how difficult it is for a corrupt people, or for a people accustomed to arbitary power, to preserve liberty when they have gained it; and that it very seldom occurs that a republic or a monarchy is well founded from the beginning, or reformed on the basis of its old institutions, except by one man, on whose mind and guidance the whole depends;[*] but for their maintenance when formed, or reformed, they depend upon the vigilance and ability of the many.

These discourses are divided into three books; the first relates to the principles followed by the Roman people in their internal affairs; the second to the course they pursued in the augmentation of their empire; the third to miscellaneous subjects of peace and war, and the proper policy and conduct of public men in various contingencies. His conclusions, drawn from the assumed identity of the circumstances of the ancient and modern Italian republics, may not be always trustworthy, and his advice to his countrymen is often tinged with the lax political morality which

---

[*] Montesquieu makes the same remark: "In the infancy of states, it is the great men who form the institutions; afterwards, it is the institutions that form the great men."

was the vice of the age. But, in the judgment of Hallam, the discourses "contain more sound and deep thinking on the spirit of small republics than could be found in any preceding writer that has descended to us; more probably, in a practical sense, than the 'Politics' of Aristotle, though not so comprehensive;" and Hallam considers that "few political treatises can even now be read with more advantage." *

BODIN.
(1530—1596.)

Towards the close of the same century was published Bodin's remarkable Treatise on a Republic; the first edition in French, in 1576, the second in Latin, with many additions, in 1586. Hallam has given an analysis of it in his History of Literature,† and agrees in the opinion of Dugald Stewart (Dissertation on the Progress of Philosophy, p. 40), that "no political writer of the period contributed more to facilitate and guide the researches of his successors." His "extraordinary reach of learning and reflection" enabled him to accumulate, in the course of his long work, many just and valuable observations on the first principles of society and government. His book was used by lecturers both in London and Cambridge, and is believed to be the source of the larger views of

---

* Hallam's History of Literature, Vol i, pp. 398—401. Edit. 1843.
† Vol. ii, pp. 51—69.

politics which gathered strength during the eventful 17th century.*

The chapters of greatest interest in the present day are those on "The Objects of Political Society," on "The Origin of the Commonwealth," and on "The Rise and Fall of States." He considers the object of political society to be the greatest good of every citizen, which is that of the whole state. His view of the origin of civil society is that, as the family was an association of many persons under one head, so the commonwealth was an association of many families submitting to one chief; but the latter association was brought about, not, as Aristotle thought, by agreement, but by force. Ambition and covetousness having led to wars, men were ready to give up a portion of their natural liberty, to live under the power of one who could protect them.

In reviewing the causes of the rise and fall of states, and the changes that occur in the three different forms of government, monarchy, aristocracy, and democracy—at times natural, gradual, and beneficial; at times violent and injurious, according as wisdom and foresight, or the contrary, have predominated in the process—he speaks strongly against the "vain" attempts that had been made, as by Lycurgus, in his institutions for Sparta, to produce and perpetuate a rigid system of political and social equality

---

* Hallam's History of Literature, Vol. ii, p. 51, note. Also, Cambridge Characteristics and Studies in the 17th Century, by J. B. Mullinger, B.A. Macmillan, 1867, p. 20.

among the members of the conquering race. Bodin compares the results with what would happen "if a man were to mix barley, wheat, oats, millet, pulse, in one heap together; for, in such case, he would make each individual seed and the whole heap together unprofitable and useless."* He argues, that as order is suitable and desirable in everything, so is it especially in the state (republicâ), in which all orders and degrees should be united and connected the one with the other, the highest with the lowest, and the intermediate with the other two—the different orders of the nobility with the different ranks of the commonalty. He says that this is the only arrangement conformable to nature; that in the endeavour to establish any other a violence must be done to the laws of nature, and that the arguments by which such deviations from nature's laws are supported "are like spiders' webs, which are, indeed, subtle and beautifully made, and are capable of entangling small flies, but the stronger creatures easily break through them."†

Bodin was not exempt from the errors of his own time; as, among others, that pure monarchy was the best form of government, and that there were cases in which the judge should obey the direction of the sovereign. Nevertheless, in Hallam's opinion, two names alone among the writers on political philosophy could be compared with his—Aristotle and

---

* Joan. Bodini, De Republicâ, Libri Sex, Franciæ, 1591, p. 553.
† Ibid., p. 1086.

Machiavelli. "Without pretending that Bodin was equal to the former in acuteness and sagacity, we may say that the experience of two thousand years, and the maxims of reason and justice, suggested or corrected by the Gospel and its ministers, by the philosophers of Greece and Rome, and by the civil law, gave him advantages, of which his judgment and industry fully enabled him to avail himself."* Hallam ranks Machiavelli's Discourses of less value as a study than Bodin's Republic; and comparing him with Montesquieu, he regards Bodin and Montesquieu, in the province of political theory, as "the most philosophical of those who have read so deeply, the most learned of those have thought so much;" both in advance of their age; both just, benevolent, and sensible of the great object of civil society, and both aware that "the basis of the philosophy of man is to be laid in the records of his past existence."†

BACON.
(1561—1622.)

Turning now our chief attention to the political writers of our own country, it is to be remarked that they had the advantage of possessing as their guide the great body of ancient law and tradition, out of

---

* Hallam's History of Literature, Vol. ii, p. 68.
† Ibid., pp. 68, 69.

which the institutions of their country had arisen, and which was regarded with so much veneration.*

Bacon was the first of our leading minds who took a large view of political subjects, and endeavoured to inform public opinion upon them. And although his historical researches, and his reflections on the times immediately preceding his own and on those in which he lived—" times that were rough, and full of mutations, and rare accidents"—did not give birth in his mind to any formal treatise upon politics, yet his dissertations (in his celebrated Essays, first published in 1597) on " The true Greatness of Kingdoms and Estates," on " Empire," on " Nobility," and on " Factions," form a body of profound thought on the general principles of human nature and of government.

Bacon points out that the elements of the true greatness of kingdoms and estates are to be found in the greatness of the individual men; in the disposition of the people, their welfare and prosperity; in good government, and wise institutions and laws; in freedom, and in a martial spirit. The people whose " ordinances, constitutions, and customs " favour the development of those elements, " sow greatness to their posterity and succession."

On the other hand, although among counsellors and statesmen " there be found, though rarely, those who can make a small state great, there will be found a great many who are so far from being able to make a

---

* Blakey's Political Literature, Vol. ii, p. 422.

small state great, that their gift lieth the other way—to bring a great and flourishing state to ruin and decay."

On this, Archbishop Whately remarks, in his Annotations to his Edition of Bacon (London, 1858, p. 115), that "by extending, as Bacon does, our view over many countries and through several ages, we may distinctly perceive the tendencies in those directions which would have escaped a more confined research." This research, he contends, shows that, although many facts prove that it is the design of the Creator that mankind should advance not only as individuals but communities, yet, in the moral and political world, wars, civil dissensions, tyrannical government, unwise laws, "operate more or less towards the frustration of this general design, and the retardation, or even reversal, of the course of improvement."

The object of the Essays above mentioned is therefore to point out how the errors are to be avoided which lead to bad government; and in so doing, Bacon takes his examples quite as frequently from Greek and Roman experiences as from those of the Italian republics, of France, of Germany, of the Low Countries, of Spain, and of England. The great mind that gave a new and true direction to the scientific thought of the world, recognised the fact that the foundations of political philosophy were to be sought for in the experience of the free nations of antiquity, and that their experience is of value to all succeeding times. Yet even he acknowledges the difficulty of just conclusions, and the need of caution in the effort to arrive at the truth. He says of civil knowledge, that "it is conversant about a subject which is of all others the most immersed in matter and the hardliest reduced to axiom."

BELLENDEN.

Bellenden, by birth a Scotchman, became an eminent advocate in Paris, where he probably met with Bodin's work, De Republicâ. In 1615, he published in Paris his Treatise on a State or Commonwealth.* Having been invested with the honorary title of Master of the Court of Requests, by James I, he dedicated to Prince Charles the first book of his treatise "On the State of the Ancient World." He tells the prince that he sends him this work "to point out to him the sources of the first lessons of civil wisdom, which, deriving their origin from the early ages of the world, have, like rills, come down to us with perpetual accessions in their progress to the sea of history, that great record of the actions of the human race." Of this book Hallam says, that in it Bellenden seems to have taken a more comprehensive view of history, and to have reflected more philosophically upon it, than perhaps any one had done

---

* Gulielmi Bellendeni, Libri Tres, Parisiis, 1635. Dr. Parr's Edition was published in London in 1787.

K

before; and he classes him, in that particular, with Vico and Montesquieu.*

The second and third books are dedicated to Prince Henry. In the second, Bellenden treats of the duties of a prince, and of the art of government; in the third, he holds up the high examples of the Roman Senate and government to the prince and to the young members of the nobility.† Following Polybius, he describes the orders of which the Roman State, at its best period, was composed; the powers of each; the bonds that united them; the mutual checks that preserved their balance; and how, finally, liberty was lost by the transference of power, first to a few, then to one man, and then to the soldiery. He points out that when those misfortunes fell upon the state, reason lost its hold upon men's minds; moderation, law, custom, duty had no longer any power; there was neither justice, nor respect for the character and virtues of distinguished citizens, nor reverence for posterity, nor deference to the authority of the senate, nor sense of the dignity of the nation. (3rd Book, pp. 42—195.) On this book Hallam remarks, that Bellenden builds much political precept on the Roman polity, but that it has less originality and reach of thought than the first two books.

---

* Hallam's History of Literature, Vol. ii, p. 520.
† "Ut in usum publicum abeat, utilitatesque tradat juventuti patriciæ." Dedication to the Second Book.

HARRINGTON. | ALGERNON SIDNEY.
(1611—1677.) | (1620—1675.)

[Up to the early part of the 17th century, the great ancient political writers, and the few already noticed who succeeded them, were the main sources of the idea of freedom, and of just and equitable government.

Writers advocating absolute monarchy had begun about that time to disseminate their doctrines. Originating with the clergy, they were taken up by Hobbes (1651), who, although he recognised the principle that the happiness of the community was the sole final cause of government, desired to found society on the despotism either of a sovereign or an assembly. Undeterred by the great political lessons of the previous ten years, he continued to hold that "to the office of the sovereign belonged the power of levying money and soldiers when, and as much as, in his own conscience he shall judge necessary;" and "that the end of a commonwealth is particular security, which is not to be had from a great multitude, unless directed by a single judgment."*

He was followed by Filmer (1680), who maintained the duty of passive obedience to the actual sovereign, however he may have become such.†

---

* Hobbes's Leviathan, or the Matter, Form and Power of a Commonwealth, 1651. Edited by Sir William Molesworth, Bart., 1839, pp. 323; 153—156.
† Hallam's History of Literature, Vol. ii, p. 535; Vol. iii, p. 429.

But the old doctrines of freedom did not cease to animate the generation of men to whom we are indebted for the bold and firm resistance they made to the arbitrary power aimed at by Charles I, and to whom we owe the germs of many of the most salutary reforms and ameliorations of recent times, which first became subjects of discussion at the beginning of the Long Parliament.

That violent counsels by degrees got the upper hand, and led at length to despotism, is what history records of every revolution that, after having established itself on the ruins of prescriptive authority and ancient custom, has run its full course.]

While the clouds of that political convulsion were hanging over our country, the ablest minds and most patriotic hearts were engaged in endeavouring to discover the means for replacing freedom upon a secure basis.

Harrington, in his well-known but unsound and speculative work, entitled Oceana (dedicated to Cromwell), proposed to secure that object by an agrarian law, preventing the accumulation of large properties, and aiming at the establishment of a moderate aristocracy.*

Algernon Sidney, a name never to be mentioned without respect by every lover of freedom, in his learned and admirable Discourses concerning government (breathing the boldest spirit of liberty), while

---

* Edit. of 1770; London, pp. 51 and 189.

laying down the principle (as opposed to the slavish doctrines of Filmer), "that God had left to nations the liberty of setting up such governments as best pleased themselves,"* and "that all just magistratical power is from the people,"† asserts also, in accordance with the examples of all former times, that "the best governments of the world have been composed of monarchy, aristocracy, and democracy" (p. 130).

With regard to democracy he says, "I believe it can suit only with the convenience of a small town, accompanied with such circumstances as are seldom found" (p. 130). He praises the mixed form of government that had for so many years prevailed, and so widely, on the continent of Europe. "They had kings, lords, commons, diets, assemblies of estates, cortez, and parliaments, in which the sovereign power of those nations did reside, and by which they were exercised. The like was practised in Hungary, Bohemia, Sweden, Denmark, Poland; and if things are changed in some of these places within a few years, they must give better proofs of having gained by the change than are yet seen in the world, before I think myself obliged to change my opinion" (p. 131). Speaking of the ancient constitution of England, he says (p. 418), that "the English government was not ill constituted, the defects more lately observed proceeding from the change of manners and corruption of

---

* Sidney's Discourses, Edit. of 1763, p. 36, first printed in 1698.
† Page 14.

the times;" and in describing the various franchises of the counties and towns, he thus asserts the principle that these franchises were conferred as a privilege, and not claimed as a right:—

"When the nation came to be more polished, to inhabit cities and towns, and to set up several arts and trades, those who exercised them were thought to be as useful to the commonwealth as the freeholders of the country, and to deserve the same privileges. But it not being reasonable that every one should in this case do as he pleased, it was thought fit that the king, with his council (which always consisted of the "proceres" and "magnates regni"), should judge what numbers of men and what places deserved to be made corporations, or bodies politic, and to enjoy those privileges," &c. He adds, that the conferring these franchises by the ruling power on particular portions of the people "can never change the nature of the thing, so as to make that an inherent which is only a delegated power" (p. 423).

LOCKE.

(1632—1704.)

The doctrine so closely connected with the name of Locke—that "civil society must have been constituted first by a covenant of a number of men, each with each, to form a commonwealth and to be bound by a majority," was advocated, before him, by Puffendorf, Hobbes, and Spinoza, in the middle of the 17th century; but all these writers, especially the first two, inclined towards absolutism.* No one, before Locke, propounded a theory as to the foundations of civil government which gave encouragement to the notions embraced by the favourers of pure democracy in modern times. These notions took their origin from the publication of the Treatise on Civil Government, written while Locke was suffering unmerited exile in Holland, to avoid the persecution of an arbitrary court, and published shortly after his return to this country, in 1688.

That the principles advocated in that treatise received their impulse in Locke's mind from recent disappointments at the course of public affairs, as suggested by Hallam,† is made more probable by the facts of his previous history. After the failure of the Commonwealth, under Cromwell, his opinions experienced a strong reaction in favour of aristocratic institutions. Having been solicited to draw up a constitution for Carolina, he framed it in the strongest spirit of aristocracy, instituting two classes of nobility, and putting restraints upon the Press. This constitution, drawn up in 1669, and accepted in 1670, was found impracticable, and was abandoned in 1673. It is thus spoken of by Bancroft, in his History of the United States :—

---

* Hallam's History of Literature, Vol. iii, part iv, Chapter iv, sect. ii.
† Ibid., p. 438.

"The ill success of the democratic revolution in England had made Locke an enemy of popular innovations, and he cherished, therefore, what at that day were called English principles, looking to the aristocracy as the surest adversary of arbitrary power. In framing the Constitution of Carolina, he forgot the fundamental principles of practical philosophy." (Vol. ii, pp. 144, 145, London, 1837.)

After his exile to Holland, Locke's mind swayed strongly in the opposite direction; a change that gave rise to his celebrated treatise, upon which Hallam, after a full review of it, pronounces the following judgment:—

"For my own part, I must confess that in these last chapters of Locke on Government I see, what sometimes appears in his other writings, that the influence of temporary circumstances on a mind a little too susceptible of passion and resentment, had prevented that calm and patient examination of all the bearings of this extensive subject which true philosophy requires."*

The following is a summary of those principles, which I have abridged from his work, using his own words:—

"The beginning of political society depends upon the consent of the individuals to join into it, and make one society.

"When any number of men have, by the consent

---

* Hallam's History of Literature, Vol. iii, pp. 438, 439.

of every individual, made a community, they have thereby made that community a body, with a power to act as one body, which is only by the will and determination of the majority.

"The great and chief end of men's uniting into commonwealths and putting themselves under government is the preservation of their property.

"The supreme power cannot take from any man any part of his property without his own consent.

"As governments cannot be supported without great charge, it is fit every one who enjoys his share of the protection should pay out of his estate his proportion for the maintenance of it. But still it must be with his own consent; *i.e.*, the consent of the majority, giving it either by themselves or the representatives chosen by them."*

The popular formulas embodying these principles are :—

1. That a political society can only be founded by the act of the majority;
2. That taxation without representation is tyranny.

These propositions, so often refuted, are nevertheless of importance from the effects they produced and are producing at the present day. The first has often been demonstrated to be false in fact and unsound in reason; the second has been shown to be an exaggerated application of a theoretical principle, sound

---

* The Works of John Locke, Edit. 1824, Vol. iv; "Two Treatises on Government," Chapter viii, pp. 595—423.

in itself, and acted upon in the early periods of our history. In the words of Hallam, " it was even in the mouths of our kings that what concerned all should be approved by all."* But in practice it has always been subject to limitations dictated by expediency.†

Hallam observes, that neither the Revolution of 1688 nor the administration of William III could have borne the test of Locke's theory, and that it stamps with illegality every government not founded on that basis. "It has therefore," he says, "been a theory fertile in great revolutions, and perhaps pregnant with more."‡ It destroys all authority resting on prescription, and all respect for usages however consecrated by the feelings of men, by long habit, and by established custom. Accordingly, in the hands of Locke's followers, in France and in other countries, it has been used to overthrow monarchy and to supersede it by democratic republics. It has been pushed still farther, to support principles which, when reduced to practice, as they were in France and Germany in 1848, render all government impossible; and when that point has been reached the circle of revolution

---

* Hallam's Middle Ages, Vol. ii, p. 151.

† The practice is as old as the ancient Lycians. Strabo, who wrote in the early part of the 1st century, says of them, that their territory contained twenty-three cities; that they were a politic and wise people; that they were governed by an assembly which met at a stated place, and was attended by representatives from those cities. The largest sent three, those of middle size two, the smallest one. And in the same proportion (ἀνάλογον δὲ) they paid taxes, and took upon themselves the other public duties. Strabonis Geographica, Edit. Kramer, Berlin, 1852, Vol. iii, p. 145.

‡ Hallam's History of Literature, Vol iii, p. 435.

begins again, in subjection for a time to military despotism.

Hallam thus speaks of it, after passing in review its principal arguments.

"Such is in substance the celebrated treatise of Locke on Government, which, with the favour of political circumstances, and the authority of his name, became the creed of a numerous party at home; while, silently spreading the fibres from its root over Europe and America, it prepared the way for theories of political society, hardly bolder in their announcement, but expressed with more passionate ardour, from which the great resolutions of the present age have sprung."*

The liability to adopt a change of view, which has been above noticed as a characteristic of Locke's mind "under the influence," as Hallam observes "of temporary circumstances," is exemplified in the 13th chapter of that same treatise. I do not remember to have seen anywhere adverted to the fact that, in that chapter, Locke contradicts the whole theory which he has been labouring to enforce.

He is arguing (§§ 157, 158) on behalf of a reform of the parliamentary representation, rendered necessary by the decay of some towns that had formerly

---

* Hallam's History of Literature, Vol. iii, p. 438. See Appendix B as to the extension of these principles within the last fifty years, in the Constitutions of the individual States of the American Union, and its effect upon the Constitution of the United States as established by Washington. See further, as to Locke's doctrines, pp. 178, 180, 205, 228, 236.

been rich and flourishing, and had therefore sent members to Parliament, and by the rise of new ones. "These places," he says, "have a just right to be represented *which before had none; and by the same reason those cease to have a right, and to be too inconsiderable for such a privilege, which before had it.*"

There is in this proposition an entire abandonment of, and a complete contradiction to, the principles he had before laid down as the only foundation of just government, namely, the consent of the majority, and of the corollary which has been deduced from it—the right of universal suffrage—and an acknowledgment, as complete, of the principle which all the great writers of former times had laid down as the true one, namely, that admission to the franchise was a *privilege*, to be conferred by the governing power upon as many as it might be deemed most expedient, under the circumstances, to extend it to, with a view to the general good.

Burke's argument, in refutation of Locke's theory that civil society rests upon contract, and that therefore it may be dissolved at any time by a majority told by the head and another society substituted by that majority (even of one) in its place, may be thus briefly stated.

"Civil society," he says, "may possibly have been first a voluntary act, but its continuance is under a permanent standing covenant co-existing with the society, and this covenant attaches upon every individual born into that society, without any act of his own. Without their choice, all persons derive benefits from that association, and are subject to duties in consequence of those benefits. Parents find themselves, without their consent, bound by duties to their children, children to their parents, and all to that ancient order of society into which they were born. The real rights of man are the benefits he derives from that society. He has a right to protection, to justice, to the fruits of his industry, and to all the other advantages arising from a settled state of government. None, except in extreme cases which are above all rule, have a right to free themselves from the duties arising out of those primary engagements. When the extreme case occurs, the decision must be taken by those who represent the whole corporate mind of the state.

"The supposed power of acting by a majority in those extreme cases must be grounded on two principles that are mere assumptions; first, that of an incorporation produced by unanimity, and secondly, an unanimous agreement that the act of a mere majority (say of one) shall pass with them and with others as the act of the whole. Neither in France nor in England had an original or any subsequent compact of the state, expressed or implied, constituted a majority of men to be told by the head to be the acting people of their several communities.

"No legislator, at any period of the world, has willingly placed the seat of active power in the hands of the multitude; because there it admits of no control, no regulation, no steady direction whatsoever. The people are the natural control on authority; but to exercise and control together is contradictory and impossible.

"When, in 1688, our constitution had been subverted by the assumption of arbitrary power by one of its parts, the Convention Parliament—representing 'the corporate mind of the state'—was called together to replace it on its ancient foundation. In the words of the Bill of Rights, ' The Lords Spiritual and Temporal and Commons in the name of the people of England' transferred their allegiance; and a subsequent Act preserved the hereditary succession of the monarchy in the Protestant line.

"Long previously, in the Petition of Right to Charles the First, the parliament said to the king: 'Your subjects have inherited this freedom.' In the same spirit, in the Bill of Rights, the two houses declared, and required the king and queen to declare, that ' all and singular the rights and liberties asserted and declared are the true, ancient, and indubitable rights and liberties of the people of this kingdom.' From Magna Charta onwards, our constitution has claimed and asserted our liberties to be an *entailed inheritance*, derived from our forefathers, and to be transmitted to our posterity. We have thus an inheritable crown, an inheritable peerage, and a House of Commons and a people inheriting privileges, franchises, and liberties from a long line of ancestors. They claimed these great rights and liberties on no abstract principles, as 'the rights of man,' but as the rights of Englishmen, and as a patrimony derived from their forefathers."*

VICO.
(1668—1744.)

After Locke's treatise On Civil Government, published in 1688, the next systematic essay on the subject of politics, was the Philosophy of History by Jean Baptiste Vico, the earliest editions of which appeared in 1725 and 1730, making part of his famous work, the New Science.

Vico's studies at Naples, where he passed his life (during forty years professor of rhetoric, and afterwards historiographer to the king), were, he tells us in his life written by himself and prefixed to the first volume,† principally devoted to Roman law, to Plato, Tacitus, Dante, Bacon, and Grotius. In his New Science, he combated the metaphysical and political opinions of his day, and studied to place the latter on the sound basis of history. His influence as an original thinker was impaired by a fantastic method and style; but in his political work, The Philosophy

---

* Burke's Works, Vol. iii, pp. 45—56, 76—81, 305, 306; Vol. ii, pp. 331, 332, Edit. 1855.
† Principi di una Scienza Nuova di J. B. Vico, 6th Edition, 3 Vols. Milan 1816. Vita p. 7. Œuvres de J. B. Vico, par Michelet, Brux. 1840, 3 Vols. 18mo. Vol. 1, Vie de Vico, Opuscules; Vols. 2—3, L'Antique Sagesse de L'Italie; Philosophie de l'Histoire.

of History, he is considered to have anticipated subsequent writers* in the fulness and precision of his general views, which he thus sums up in page 240 of the Fifth Book of his History :—

"After having observed how societies begin over again to run the same course, let us reflect on the many points of resemblance between ancient and modern times, and we shall find reproduced, not the exact history of any one Greek or Roman state, but a kind of ideal history of the eternal laws which all nations follow in the beginning of their progress, in their decline, and in their end. Amid diversity of forms we shall recognise an identity of substance in all this course of history."

The following propositions may be taken as exemplifying the various lights in which he places his general conclusions :

1. The first kind of government is that of a sort of domestic monarchy.

This changes by degrees into an aristocracy.

The restricted territory to which an aristocracy confines itself, for the facility of government, becomes extended by the conquering spirit of democracy.

Then comes monarchy again, as a refuge from disturbances; and it is most respected in proportion to its grandeur.

---

* See Biographie Universelle, Lit. Vico. The writer of the Preface to the Milan Edition of his works says : "Montesquieu, chi ne connobbe tutto il merito, trasportò, nello " Spirito delle Leggi, "molte idee del nostro autore."

2. Sometimes, from the suspicious government of an aristocracy, the people pass to the storms of democracy, and then seek refuge in a monarchy.

3. Again, they set out from the unity of a domestic monarchy, to pass through the governments of the few, the greater number, and the whole, to return to the unity of civil monarchy.

4. The return may be expected of the same revolutions when the societies that have been destroyed recover themselves from their ruins.*

The main conclusion to which his researches and reflections lead him is:

"This New Science would not deserve the name of the uniform and eternal history of humanity, if the author has not made it plain that the characteristics observed in ancient times are reproduced, in great part, in those of the middle ages" which he has been passing in review. (Ibid.)

It is observable that Vico, in the absence in his day of the test of experience, only alludes to the mixed form of government to intimate his agreement with the conclusion of Tacitus, that if formed it could not be lasting. And the same circumstance leads him, in his brief allusion to the English monarchy, to anticipate, from its varied fortunes during his time, that its tendency was to become arbitrary, as in Poland.

It may be here noted that, after the second edition

---

* Michelet's Edit., Vol. iii, p. 207.

of the Scienza Nuova had appeared in 1730, twelve years elapsed before the publication of Hume's Essays, Moral, Political, and Literary, in 1742; and that Montesquieu's Esprit des Lois was published in 1748. A revised edition of Vico's work was published in 1744, shortly before his death.

HUME.
(1711—1776.)

Hume's brief essays on Politics a Science, The First Principles of Government, Civil Liberty, The Independence of Parliament, and Parties—making part of his collected Essays*—are coloured by the feelings and experiences of his time. Having before him the party passions and the political corruption then prevalent, he was "led to the conclusion that the world was still too young to fix many general truths in politics which would remain true to the latest posterity." Some, he thought, might be accepted, as conformable to all experience of men in society.

He does not undervalue the fact that the circumstances of the ancient world greatly differed from the modern; that the advance of the arts and sciences, and of trade and commerce, a free press, a higher standard of morals, the greater security of life and

---

* Essays, Moral, Political, and Literary, by David Hume, 1742. Longman, 1875.

property, the abolition of slavery, and other products of civilization, afford elements of stability before unknown. To these are to be added the established principles of political economy, not known in Hume's time,* but recognised by Dugald Stewart, writing in 1792,† as powerfully co-operating, with the other factors above mentioned, towards the same results.

But those circumstances do not, in his opinion, affect the conclusions that have been generally accepted regarding the main principles of human conduct and government.

After referring to the careers of republican Rome, aristocratical Venice, and Poland, and the absolute monarchy of France, and pointing out their several defects, he concludes in favour of a mixed government, and affirms "That it may be pronounced as an axiom in politics that an hereditary prince, a nobility without vassals, and a people voting by their representatives, form the best monarchy, aristocracy, and democracy." And stating the conclusion more fully, he says, that "The government which, according to common understanding, is free, is that which admits a partition of powers among several members . . . who in the usual course of administration must act by general and equal laws previously known to all. In this sense, liberty is the perfection of civil society."

The balance of power he calls "a secret in politics

---

* Smith's Wealth of Nations was not published until 1776.
† See p. 152.

fully known only in the present age." The problem is, how to adjust the balance to meet each recurring necessity as it arises. For the danger is never absent, amidst the constant mutations of power, of one of the constituent elements encroaching upon the other, " so that at one time men are jealous of monarchy, at another more jealous of popular government."

To counteract this danger, constant watchfulness is required, and due adjustments must be made in such a manner as not to impair the free and efficient action of the whole. " In the smallest court or office, the stated forms, institutions, and methods are found to be a considerable check on the natural depravity of mankind. Why should not the case be the same in public affairs?" . . . . . "Here, then, is a sufficient inducement to maintain, with the utmost zeal, in every free state, those institutions by which liberty is secured, the public good consulted, and the avarice or ambition of particular men restrained and punished." . . . . " Effects will always correspond to causes, and wise regulations in any commonwealth are the most valuable legacies that can be left to future ages." . . . . " This may teach us a lesson of moderation in all our political controversies;" and he believes, notwithstanding the violence of those controversies in his day, that " all reasonable men agree in general to preserve our mixed constitution."

MONTESQUIEU.
(1689—1755.)

The great work of Montesquieu, on The Spirit of Laws, was published in 1748, just six years after Hume's political essays. In order to make his work useful to other countries besides his own, he visited, while preparing it, Germany, Italy, Switzerland, the United Provinces, and finally England, where he stayed two years. He studied the laws and institutions of each country, and became acquainted with the prominent writers and public men in each. Burke, in his splendid eulogy of the Esprit des Lois, states that Montesquieu spent twenty years in its preparation.* In the Preface to the Paris edition of 1794 (p. 4), it is said that " He formed in London intimate relations with men of thought and acquirements, from whom he gained instruction as to the nature of the government, so as at length fully to understand it. That famous isle, that prides itself so much upon its institutions, was for him a school in which he gathered knowledge, without giving his approval to every particular."

In his chapter on the English Constitution, Montesquieu sets forth fully its chief characteristics—the separation of the legislative, executive, and judicial

---

* Burke's Works, Vol. iii, p. 113, Edit. of 1855.

powers;* the system of representation, municipal and general, and the respective power of the two houses of the legislature. He examines and approves of the reasons on which these several principles are based, and points out their superiority over other free governments, ancient and modern.

As regards the portion of the community in whom the power of voting should be vested, although perfectly acquainted with the theory of Locke—that it is an inherent right—he rejected that theory, and treated the possession of the suffrage as a matter of expediency, having for its object the obtaining from the community an enlightened and independent judgment.

He says, that in forming an opinion of political institutions "it is necessary to have regard to the particular character and circumstances of each people. He did not take his own principles from his prejudices (which were in favour of his own country), but from the nature of things." He recognises with evident regret, that the other countries of Europe, his own included, were not in the condition to adopt the mixed system which he saw in action in England. They had to be content with following the example of Solon who did not give the Athenians the best possible

---

* Sir Edward Creasy, in his work on the Rise and Progress of the English Constitution (6th Edition, London, 1862), in classifying the constitutional functions of each member of the state under three heads —1st, the deliberative ; 2nd, the administrative ; 3rd, the judicial— says : "I follow here the greatest of all writers on the subject of political institutions—Aristotle." (Page 7.)

laws, but the best which they could bear. But "the more those mixed principles are anywhere in vigour, the more stable is the government. It is from the legitimate distribution and the suitable division of these different species of powers that the greatest perfection of political liberty arises. Thence proceeds true equality;" by which he understands "that happy equilibrium which makes all the citizens equally subjected to the laws, and equally interested in observing them."

This same principle is strongly enforced by Machiavelli in his remarkable letter to Leo X, on a scheme of reform for the State of Florence, in which he says: "Those who model a commonwealth must take such provisions as may assign a place to three sorts of men—the high, the middle, and the low.* Of which passage Mr. Adams, in his defence of the American Constitution (referred to in Appendix B), speaks as "that great truth, that eternal principle, without the knowledge of which every speculation upon government must be imperfect, and every scheme of a commonwealth essentially defective."

Each of the constitutional elements of the mixed form of government—the monarchical, the aristocratic, and the democratic—being in itself so strong, Montesquieu perceives—following Hume—that the just balance can only be preserved by the practice of moderation, "which is the soul of a government of this kind."

---

* Machiavelli's Works, Vol. v, p. 246.

In the course of the chapter on the English Constitution, he refers frequently to the institutions of Greece and Rome "of which the English Constitution supplies the defects." .... "That fine system," he says, "was found in the woods. It was worked out in several of its main outlines by our German ancestors."*

DUGALD STEWART.
(1753—1828.)

The chapter on the "Use and Abuse of General Principles in Politics," in Dugald Stewart's noble work, The Philosophy of the Human Mind (1792),† enlarged the sphere of the political thought of the time, and led it towards the more enlightened convictions which bore fruit in the next generation. He was among the first to perceive how greatly the then newly-published doctrines of Adam Smith, on the Nature and Causes of the Wealth of Nations, would promote the well-being of a country, and "extend its political prospects."

---

* Tacitus, De Moribus Germanorum, Chapters vii, xi, xii, xiv. On this subject Sir Edward Creasy remarks: "The main stream of our nation is Germanic. The institutions of our Germanic ancestors commanded the anxious interest of the master minds of ancient Rome. Those same institutions are the first subjects to which the inquirer into our laws and our political organization must bend his thoughts. They have, indeed, been greatly modified by the other elements with which they have been mingled here, but they have exercised more influence than any others. The Germania of Tacitus is equally a handbook for the student of modern, and for the student of ancient history. It thus demonstrates the unity of all history." (Rise and Progress of the English Constitution, p. 10.) See further on this subject, Appendix C.

† Edition of 1802, Vol. i, chapter 4, section 8.

And he cordially recognised all that was good in the speculations of the French economists, in so far as they "searched for the causes of national prosperity and national improvement in those arrangements which daily observations show to be favourable to the prosperity and the improvement of individuals."

On the other hand, he pronounced strongly against "those Utopian plans of government" of Locke and others, "which have, at different times, been offered to the world." " Of these plans," he says, "by far the greater number proceed on the supposition, that the social order is entirely the effect of human art; and that wherever this order is imperfect, the evil may be traced to some want of foresight on the part of the legislator; or to some inattention of the magistrate to the complicated structure of that machine of which he regulates the movements. The projects of reform, therefore, which such plans involve, are, in general, well entitled to all the ridicule and contempt they have met with; inasmuch as they imply an arrogant and presumptuous belief in their authors, of the superiority of their own political sagacity to the accumulated wisdom of former ages."

He was impressed, as fully as Hume, with the advantages which modern nations derive from the vast number and variety of their inventions, from a free press, and from the rapid circulation of knowledge; and he was possessed with an ardent anticipation that the combined influences of those modern powers would tend to the removal of the obstacles which the prejudices and vices of men had so long opposed to the progress of truth, freedom, and virtue.

These considerations did not lead him to undervalue the search after the great principles of government, "of which the most extensive experience alone would put us in possession." They were to be found in "the known principles of human nature, combined with the particular circumstances of the time;" in those principles which we obtain "from an examination of the human constitution, and of the general laws which regulate the course of human affairs, and which are certainly the result of a much more extensive induction than any of the inferences drawn from the history of actual establishments."

The numerous speculative writers on government in the two centuries before Dugald Stewart's time aimed at recommending either an absolute monarchy, an aristocracy, or a democracy,* and were therefore open to his remark, that, so far as their reasons were founded merely on the experience of past times, they were unphilosophical and inconclusive, inasmuch as they could necessarily take no account of the great "modern power of public opinion, and its ascendant in human affairs which it had never possessed before."

To this power, arising from the liberty of the press, and now greatly increased by the many other inventions and improvements of more recent times, he looked for a sufficient check on any dangerous

---

* For the writers of the 17th century, see Hallam's History of Literature, Vol. iii, part 4, section 2.

advance of extreme opinions in any direction. Referring to the remark of Hobbes, that "Democracy is nothing but an aristocracy of orators, interrupted sometimes by the temporary monarchy of a single orator," he considers "that one of the greatest advantages to be expected from the liberty of the press is, the effect that it must necessarily have in diminishing the influence of popular eloquence, both by curing men of those prejudices upon which it operates, and by subjecting it to the irresistible control of enlightened opinion." And in proportion as these prospects of the progress of reason, the diffusion of knowledge, and the consequent improvement of mankind are realised, he anticipates "that the political history of the world will be regulated by steady and uniform courses, and the philosopher will be enabled to form probable conjectures with respect to the future course of human affairs."

The spectacle of the result of the abuses of aristocratical and monarchical power all over Europe, at the time when Dugald Stewart wrote, did not carry away his philosophical mind into any condemnation of their principles. He perceived that then, partly as the result of those abuses, partly "in consequence of the progress of commerce and philosophy, the aristocratical influence was rapidly declining." But he thought, also, that "no well-wisher to mankind would be disposed to accelerate its decline." He anticipated a time when it might be dispensed with, when "the true principles of political economy are completely understood and acknowledged by the world." Doubtless he applied the term political economy in a much wider than a mere material sense, since he acknowledges the value of an hereditary aristocracy in counteracting the influence of wealth, and consequently in tending to promote all the qualities that elevate human life. His ideal of government is expressed in the following words: "Governments are more or less perfect in proportion to the greater or smaller numbers of individuals to whom they afford the means of cultivating their intellectual and moral powers, and whom they admit to live together on a liberal footing of equality." . . . . And therefore " to the statesman is assigned the sublime office of seconding the benevolent intentions of Providence in the administration of human affairs, by diffusing as widely as possible among his fellow-citizens the advantages of the social union."

He does not omit to point out that " the danger of sudden and rash innovations cannot be too strongly inculcated." . . . . " But it is possible, also, to fall into the opposite extreme, and to bring upon society the very evils we are anxious to prevent, by an obstinate opposition to those gradual and necessary reformations which the genius of the times demands. The violent revolutions which at different times have convulsed modern Europe have arisen from this cause." . . . . " The perfection, therefore, of political wisdom does not consist in indiscriminate zeal against reforms, but in a gradual and prudent accommodation of established institutions to the varying opinions, manners, and circumstances of mankind."

In his Lectures on Government (1804), Dugald Stewart deals with 1st, the simple forms, 2nd, mixed governments. Pointing out that the great object of the theory of government is to separate and properly distribute the legislative, judicial, and executive powers, so as to guard against the abuses to which they might otherwise be liable, he says that " these ends can only be accomplished by a mixed government; that is, by a system of policy that would combine the simple forms in such a manner as to correct the inconveniences which, in their separate states, they seem all to threaten." When these powers are thus united, the political order which arises from such a combination may be compared, as they were by Cicero,* to the harmony resulting from the different instruments and voices, and the high, low, and intermediate sounds of a musical concert. These conditions are satisfied by the English Constitution. He adds, that one of his leading motives for those lectures was his desire to " illustrate and enforce the duties of patriotism, which, among those we owe to our fellow-creatures, certainly hold a most distinguished rank."†

---

* De Rep., Book ii, ch. 42.
† The Collected Works of Dugald Stewart, edited by Sir William Hamilton, 1856. Vol. ix, pp. 351, 459.

PITT.	FOX.	BURKE.
(1759—1806.)	(1748—1806.)	(1730—1797.)

The three great statesmen of the latter part of the last century, while fully agreeing as to the theoretical excellence of the British Constitution, as settled by the Revolution of 1688, were equally conscious of the defects which had been imported into it by the undue influence of the crown and the corruption of public opinion. They differed as to the mode and time in which its reform should be undertaken.

PITT.—In his Notice of a Motion on the Present State of the Representation of the Commons of England, in May, 1782, Pitt prefaced his proposals by the assertion that " That beautiful form of government which had made us the envy and admiration of mankind, in which the people were entitled to hold so distinguished a share, was so far departed from its original purity, as that its representatives ceased, in a great degree, to be connected with the people."* And he referred to his father, Lord Chatham, as having said, some years before, that " Without reform, this nation, with the best capacities for grandeur and happiness of any on the face of the earth, must be confounded in the mass of those whose liberties were lost in the corruption of the people." Mr. Pitt proceeded

---

* Speeches of William Pitt. 6 vols. London, 1806, p. 27.

to say that the defects in the representation had given reason to apprehend the most alarming consequences to the constitution; and he recalled the previous efforts at reform that had failed in consequence of the too great influence of the crown. He asserted that a spirit of unanimity in favour of reform had sprung up in every part of the kingdom, and he proposed an inquiry and a report to the government on the best means of carrying into execution a moderate and substantial reform in the representation of the people. He intimated that he shared the opinion of those who thought that "the best means of effecting a more near relation between the representatives and the people was to take from the decayed and corrupt boroughs a part of their members, and add them to the places which have a greater interest and stake in the country." (Vol. i, pp. 31, 32.)

He found the House of Commons averse even to an inquiry. Nevertheless he returned to the subject the next year, and in May, 1783, proposed three resolutions :—1st. That measures should be taken to prevent bribery and expense at elections. 2nd. The disfranchisement of boroughs where the majority of voters were convicted of corruption by a committee of the House of Commons. 3rd. An addition to the knights of the shire. It is observable that, in deference probably to the strength of the opposition, there is no attempt to deal with the decayed boroughs. He urged, that " The more he revered the venerable part of the constitution—the more he wished to secure its duration—the greater he felt the necessity of guarding against its decay."

On the subject of the franchise, he said, that "Some* proposed to give this right of voting, indiscriminately, to all the inhabitants of the kingdom. . . . . But if this doctrine should prevail, nearly one-half of the people must in fact be slaves; . . . . for all those who vote for an unsuccessful candidate cannot, in the strictness of this doctrine, be said to be represented in parliament, and therefore they are governed by laws to which they give not their assent, either in person or by representatives." . . . . That the member, "when once chosen, ought to consider himself the representative of the people at large," does not invalidate the above conclusion. "Universal suffrage," in his opinion, "was a speculative proposition, which may be good in theory, but absurd and chimerical to reduce to practice."

The resolutions were lost by a large majority. (Vol. i, pp. 74—80.)

In April, 1785, Mr. Pitt again called attention to the question of the reform of the representation. He reminded the House that since the period of Edward I, which was the first time when they could trace distinct descriptions of men in the representation, the doctrine of change was clearly understood. The representation in counties was not uniform; the total number of members frequently varied. From the

---

* Referring to those who had adopted the principles of Locke.

time of Edward I to Charles II there were few reigns in which the representation did not undergo a change. Of boroughs which used formerly to send members 72 had fallen into decay, and had been disfranchised. After the Restoration, 36 petitioned to be restored, and their prayer was granted; the remainder did not petition, and were left without their franchises. (Vol. i, p. 226.)

The limited and tentative nature of Mr. Pitt's proposals in this bill indicated the strength of the borough interest in the House of Commons. Decayed boroughs were to be purchased, with their consent, by parliament, and their members distributed among the counties; and other small boroughs were to have power to surrender their franchises for a consideration, and their right to return members was to be transferred to populous and flourishing towns. Copyholders were to have the franchise in the counties. But the opinion of parliament was adverse to even this mild measure; and the rising storm of the French Revolution prevented the subject of the reform of the representation from being again introduced until it was revived by Mr. Grey in 1793. On this occasion Pitt, while declaring himself as desirous as ever to see the needful reforms effected, considered the time inopportune. The efforts to propagate the principles of the French Revolution had alarmed the nation. "The societies," he said, "demanding reform, brought forward a claim that could be resolved into nothing but a deduction from French principles—that which is termed the will of the majority, the will of the multitude. Under a pretence of centering all authority in the will of the many, it established the worst sort of despotism." (Vol. ii, p. 156.)

When Mr. Grey again brought forward his motion in 1797, disclaiming at the same time French principles, Pitt opposed it on the ground that he did not think the motion could be separated from the objects of the societies (Vol. iii, p. 128); and although Fox, who had strenuously supported his great rival Pitt in all his endeavours to obtain acceptance for his proposals for reform, also supported this motion, he found himself, together with all the friends of rational reformation, confounded, in the opinion of the country, with the advocates of the wild doctrines of the French Revolution.*

During the great struggle into which, in 1794, the country was forced, first with France, and for a time with the whole of Europe, and which lasted until 1815, the question of the reform of the representation remained naturally in abeyance. Lord John Russell, by whom it was taken up again in May 1819, and in April 1822, found the country still unprepared for it. But the subsequent French Revolution in 1830, which aimed at establishing constitutional monarchy in that country on a firmer basis, supplied the impulse that enabled Earl Grey to introduce, and in 1832 to carry, the great measure which will be for ever associated

---

* Burke's Speech on Economic Reform. Vol. ii of his Speeches, p. 55.

with his name, and which gave effect to, and by the aid of a wider experience extended, the principles by which the enlightened patriotism of Pitt and Fox had vainly sought to enlarge the bounds, and strengthen the foundation of the constitution.

Fox.—In his speech on introducing his Motion for considering the State of the Nation, in January 1784, Fox thus expressed himself on the subject of the constitution. " The theory of our constitution consisted in checks and oppositions; in one part of our legislature bearing up against and controlling another, but it was the prudence of good men to moderate the temper of the constitution, and on this practice a happy medium has been hit upon at the glorious era of the Revolution, temperate and accommodating, the good effects of which we have experienced for near a century."* (Vol. ii of Speeches, p. 321.)

Holding this view and " regarding it as one of the chief excellences of the constitution that it involved a renovating principle in itself" (ibid., p. 172), and being as zealous as the best men in his age to correct its abuses, he nevertheless pronounced strongly against the doctrines then becoming popular, by which all other power of the state would be overpowered by the will of the majority. In his speech on Mr. Grey's Motion for a Reform in Parliament, in May 1797, (Vol. vi, p. 363) he says, "I always deprecated universal suffrage." . . . " I do not think that you augment

---

* Speeches of the Right Honorable Charles James Fox. 4 vols. Bohn, London, 1815.

the deliberative body of the people by counting all the heads, but that in truth you confer on individuals* by this means the power of drawing forth numbers who, without deliberation, would act implicitly on their will. My opinion is, that the best reform is that which shall bring into activity the greatest number of independent voters, and that that is defective which would bring forth those whose situation and condition take from them the power of deliberation."

A similar opinion, expressed by Fox in 1800, is recorded in the life of Sir James (then Mr.) Mackintosh, from the diary of a friend. Mr. Mackintosh mentioned that, upon asking Fox's opinion of what he had observed of the necessary complexity of all free governments, from the various elements out of which they must arise and the various interests with which they must be charged, Fox said that nothing certainly could be more true; nor anything more foolish than the doctrines of the advocates for simpler forms of government.†

And of his claim upon the confidence and respect of posterity for his political conclusions, Sir James Mackintosh thus speaks in his eloquent exposition of the lofty and splendid qualities of Fox's character: "The measures which he supported or opposed

---

* An allusion to the leaders of the republican clubs who had made themselves so conspicuous in France, and an anticipation of the "wire-pullers" of the present day.

† Memoirs of the Life of Sir James Mackintosh, edited by his son Robert James Mackintosh, Esq. Second Edition. In 2 vols. London, 1836. Vol. i, p. 109.

may divide the opinions of posterity; . . . but he will most certainly command the unanimous reverence of future generations by his pure sentiments towards the commonwealth, by his zeal for the civil and religious rights of all men, by his liberal principles favourable to mild government, to the unfettered exercise of the human faculties, and to the progressive civilization of mankind; by his ardent love for a country of which the well-being and greatness were indeed inseparable from his own glory, and by his profound reverence for that free constitution which he was universally admitted to understand better than any other man of his age, both in an exactly legal, and in a comprehensively philosophical sense."*

A passage in Fox's History of the Early Part of the reign of James II shows that, while having the strongest sympathy for freedom, he sided with those who would protect it from the tyranny, either of the few or the many. In his description of the popular party in opposition to Charles I, he says that "Many of their leaders were greatly versed in ancient as well as modern learning, and were even enthusiastically attached to the great names of antiquity; but they never conceived the wild project of assimilating the government of England to that of Athens, of Sparta, or of Rome. They were content with applying to the English Constitution, and to the English laws, the spirit of liberty which had animated and rendered illustrious the ancient republics. They had no

---

* Ibidem, p. 325.

thought of a republic in its modern sense, the radical defects of which, as wanting in freedom, can only be mitigated by the genius of a Cromwell" (pp. 3, 19).*
And in his Address to the Electors of Westminster, 1793, in the midst of the excitement of the French

---

* The following old poem, from the Luttrell collection of "Broadsides,"[a] of the probable date of 1660, and manifestly by an admirer of the Long Parliament in its best period, so fully illustrates Fox's sentiments in the above paragraph, that it may be permitted to add it here. It was given in the Athenæum of March 14th, 1857.

ENGLAND'S VOTE FOR A FREE ELECTION IN A FREE PARLIAMENT.

Great God of Nations, and their Right,
  By whose high Auspice Brittain stands
  So long, though first 'twas built on Sands,
And oft had sunk, but for Thy might,

In her own Mainland-storms and Seas :
  Be present to her now as then,
  And let not proud and factious men
Oppose Thy will with what they please.

Our Free full Senate's to be made ;
  O put it to the publick voice
  To make a legal worthy choice,
Excluding such as would invade

The Commonwealth. Let whom we name
  Have Wisdome, Foresight, Fortitude,
  Be more with Faith then Face endu'd ;
And study Conscience above Fame.

Such, as not seek to get the Start
  In State, by Faction, Power, or Bribes,
  Ambition's Bands. But move the *Tribes*
By Virtue, Modesty, Desert.

Such as to Justice will adhere,
  Whatever great one it offend ;
  And from the embracèd Truth not bend
For Envy, Hatred, Gifts, or Fear.

That by their Deeds will make it known
  Whose Dignity they do sustain ;
  And Life, State, Glory, all they gain,
Count it Great Brittain's, not their own.

[a] In 3 vols. folio, now in the British Museum. The poem is in Vol. ii, A to H.

Revolution, he referred to the terms of an Amendment which he had recently moved to the Address to the Crown in the House of Commons, in which he expressed the desire of the House to check the tendency to arbitrary proceedings on the part of the government, but at the same time " to assure His Majesty of their most zealous attachment to the excellent constitution of this free country, and their sense of the immeasurable blessings which are derived from it, and their unshaken determination to maintain and preserve it."

BURKE.—In his defence of the doctrine of the constitution, as established in 1688, Burke said that " The excellences of the British Constitution had already exercised and exhausted the labours of the best thinkers and the most eloquent writers that the world had yet seen."* . . . It was the result of the thoughts of many minds, in many ages. It is a very

---

  Such the old Bruti, Decii were,
   The Cippi, Curtii, who did give
   Themselves for Rome: and would not live
  As men good only for a year.

  Such were the great Camilli too,
   The Fabii, Scipio's; that still thought
   No work at price enough was bought
  That for their country they could do:

  And to her honour so did knit,
   As all their Acts were understood
   The Sinews of the Publick Good,
  And they themselves one soul with it.

  These men were truly Magistrates;
   These neither practised Force, nor Forms,
   Nor did they leave the helm in storms;
  And such they are make happy States.

 * Appeal from the New to the Old Whigs, 1791. Burke's Works, 4 vols. London, 1855, Vol. iii, p. 12.

complicated system, and therefore to be handled with caution. "Our constitution stands on a nice equipoise, with steep precipices and deep waters upon all sides. In removing it from a dangerous leaning towards one side there may be risk of oversetting it on the other. Every project of a material change in a government so complicated as ours, combined at the same time with external circumstances still more complicated, is a matter full of difficulties; in which a considerate man will not be too ready to decide, or an honest man too ready to promise. . . . It is the business of the speculative philosopher to mark the proper ends of government; it is the business of the politician, who is the philosopher in action, to find out proper means towards those ends, and to employ them with effect."* . . . "With a disposition to improve he should show an ability to preserve."† And in aiming at improvements "he would vary his means to secure the unity of his end; when the equipoise of the vessel may be endangered by overloading it on one side, he would carry the weight of his reasons to that which may preserve its equipoise."‡

At the time of the French Revolution the abuses and oppressions of the old monarchical and aristocratical governments on the Continent had been so great, that many of the finest intellects in this country

---

* Thoughts on the Cause of the Present Discontents. Vol. i of Works, pp. 368—376.
† Reflections on the Revolution in France. Vol. ii of Works, p. 428.
‡ Ibid., p. 518.

were carried away in ardent hope and expectation of a new era of freedom and national well-being that was to arise out of the doctrines then promulgated by the French philosophers. The events of the Revolution (to use the words of Sir James Mackintosh) "only too effectually refuted" those doctrines, and dispelled the expectations which he, among others, had at one time built upon them. Burke from the first saw deeper into the principles at work in France, and gave all his marvellous energies to exposing their fallacies.

The real foundations of civil society and government upon which, if the responsible classes do their duty, the well-being of a community in its highest sense is constructed and maintained, are expounded by Burke throughout a large portion of his works and speeches, but nowhere more fully than in his Thoughts on French Affairs, in his Reflections on the Revolution in France, and in his Appeal from the New to the Old Whigs.* He shows that the abettors of the shallow theories that overturned the old monarchical government of France proceeded upon the assumption that, in the effort to attain a better order of things, there was no middle way between the despotism of a monarchy and the despotism of a multitude. They acted as if "they had never heard of a monarchy directed by laws, controlled and balanced by the great hereditary wealth

---

* Vols. ii and iii, Burke's Works.

and hereditary dignity of a nation; and both again controlled by a judicious check from the reason and feeling of the people at large, acting by a suitable and permanent organ." They seemed to think it impossible that anyone "could honestly prefer such a mixed and tempered government to either of the *extremes.*" They were led to regard "as a truth universally acknowledged, that a pure democracy is the only tolerable form into which human society can be thrown;" they were unaware that "the *extreme* of liberty ought not to obtain anywhere; because extremes, in every point which relates either to our duties or satisfactions in life, are destructive both to virtue and enjoyment. Liberty must be limited in order to be possessed."* There may be small communities "in which the purely democratic form will become necessary; there may be some (very few, and very particularly circumstanced) in which it would be clearly desirable. This he did not take to be the case of France, or of any other great country. Until now we have seen no examples of considerable democracies."† And when adopted as the polity of a large community, in which strong divisions of opinion may be expected to be found, the oppression of the minority " will extend to far greater numbers," and be exercised more harshly than is likely to be the case under the government of one man. The tendency of a pure democracy is "to

---

* Letter to the Sheriffs of Bristol. Ibid., vol. ii, p. 30.
† Reflections, vol. ii, p. 396.

degenerate into an oligarchy;" under it there is a less prospect for a people to rise into a state of true freedom; "you can better engraft any description of republic on a monarchy than anything of monarchy upon the republican forms. The fact is so historically."*
And of this there is no greater example than the English Constitution which, in its gradual growth, has become compounded of all that is best in the three simple forms.† The two great countries which, in Burke's time, had adopted democratic institutions, are now able to show a century's experience of them. I have put together in the Appendix, (A and B,) some observations on each.

One of the most conspicuous acts of Burke's public life was his resistance to the dictation of his constituents at Bristol. On that memorable occasion he originated a principle that has been recognised as among the most valuable of our constitutional usages. Speaking of himself in the third person he thus describes it. "He was the first man who, on the hustings at a popular election, rejected the authority of instructions from constituents; and who, in any place, has argued so fully against it. Perhaps the discredit into which that doctrine of compulsive instructions

---

* Reflections, vol ii, p. 397.
† It has been suggested by Mr. John Morley that the English Constitution, which has been described as "not a creation but a *growth*," would be more properly characterised as "the result of deliberate human effort acting in accordance with national character and favouring circumstances." (Vol. ii, p. 180, of Mr. Morley's Dissertations on Rousseau, referred to in pp. 217, 222.)

under our constitution is since fallen, may be due, in a great degree, to his opposing himself to it in that manner, and on that occasion.*

In the speech itself, to which he alludes, delivered at Bristol before the election in 1780, he urges that "If we do not, by a fair, indulgent, and gentlemanly behaviour to our representatives, give confidence to their minds, and a liberal scope to their understandings; if we do not permit our members to act upon a very enlarged view of things, we shall at length infallibly degrade our national representation into a confused and scuffling bustle of local agency. When the popular member is narrowed in his ideas, and rendered timid in his proceedings, the service of the crown will be the sole nursery of statesmen. . . . Then the monopoly of mental power will be added to the power of all other kinds that it possesses. On the side of the people there will be nothing but impotence, for ignorance is impotence; narrowness of mind is impotence; timidity is itself impotence, and makes all other qualities that go along with it impotent and useless."†

There being no longer the boroughs under the influence of the crown (or of individuals), alluded to in the above paragraph, through which men who had been rejected by the exactions of constituencies might continue their services to the public, the result in the

---

* An Appeal from the New to the Old Whigs, p. 26.
† Speech at Bristol previous to his election in 1780. Vol. ii of Works, p. 130.

present day of the dictation of constituencies would be to drive men of jealous honour and individual character from public life, or to prevent them from entering it.

The result of that habit of dictation may be now studied in the representation in the individual States of the American Union, and in that of the United States, the leading facts of which I have given in an Appendix (B); and they are not such as to commend themselves to the higher sense and feeling and foresight of the public of this country.

The line of conduct which Burke commends to constituencies is that of a general agreement on principles with their representative, and a candid and liberal consideration of the *whole tenour* of his conduct. To attempt to impose mere obsequiousness and flexibility is a fault radically ruinous to the representative character and to the state.* Elsewhere he describes what should be expected of a good member of parliament. He should feel himself bound to look beyond local interests to those of the nation; to bear in mind that the nation itself is but a part of a great empire, and that the several interests of the nation and the empire are various, multiform, and intricate. Those wide-spread interests must be considered, compared, and, if possible, reconciled. To enable him to discharge such duties it is obvious that a large discretion

---

* Speech at Bristol previous to his election in 1780. Vol. ii of Works, pp. 129—131.

must be left to a representative, as a member of a deliberate assembly.*

Burke's analysis of the principles on which the idea of monarchy rested, and of the reasons in favour of a Church establishment, are so expanded by the energy of his convictions and the riches of his eloquence, that nothing but a short summary of them is here possible.

Of monarchy he says, that the idea has been common to all ages and nations, and is founded on our natural impulses of respect and reverence. To respect the office and person of the sovereign is among the oldest and most universal feelings of mankind. This reverence is yielded willingly and freely, with the generous loyalty that " dignifies obedience," and raises him who yields it in his own esteem. " We naturally cherish and cultivate those inbred sentiments as the faithful guardians and the true supporters of all liberal and manly morals." By reverencing the sovereign, and thus embodying our institutions in a person, we also engage the affections on the side of the commonwealth. We therefore immensely strengthen our institutions when we are able to bestow the natural affections of love, veneration, admiration, and attachment, on the person who represents to us the idea of the state. So strong is the natural feeling of veneration for the office of the sovereign, that it has often survived the shock of the vices of the temporary

---

* Burke's Works, Vol. iii, pp. 27—29.

occupants of the throne. When on the other hand, to the respect for office is added the claim of high personal qualities, the nation's tribute of affection and attachment is offered in full measure to the sovereign, who is the worthy embodiment of its dignity, grandeur, and power.

The loss is great to the nations whose social system does not permit them to possess a living embodiment of their national dignity. Deprived of a legitimate object to which their natural feelings of veneration can attach themselves, they are led to expend those feelings on objects of a lower kind.*

The argument for a Church establishment rests, according to Burke, on the following basis. The common nature and common relation of men require the institution of civil society. Without civil society man could not by any possibility arrive at the perfection of which his nature is capable. It must therefore be acceptable to the Divine Being who is the Institutor, and Author, and Protector of civil society, that national homage should be rendered to Him; that, as our nature is to be perfected by our virtue, men bound together in civil society should take the necessary means for its perfection. It is incumbent on the nation in its corporate capacity, to protect the means provided for that purpose.

In this country, the means for this corporate fealty

---

* Reflections on the Revolution in France; Burke's Works, Vol. ii, pp. 348—356.

and homage have been provided by individuals, and placed under the guardianship of the state. These means have afforded the opportunities of the public recognition of the Sovereign of Sovereigns in buildings, by public acts of worship according to dignified and suitable forms; by instruction; by the ministrations of consolation and hope, in every parish of the kingdom. These means thus assigned for these purposes by individuals, from time to time, during the course of more than a thousand years, are the inheritance of the nation, and are especially the inheritance of the poor. They provide a body of men, the object of whose education and training is to qualify them to be not only the teachers, but the friends and guides of the poor, and the promoters of the national civilization. That body of men, commanding also by their cultivation and position the attention and respect of the rich, are the instruments by which in that class the national standard of morals and religion is sustained and elevated. In the maintenance of that standard at its highest point among the rich, no class has a greater interest than the poor; for no class derives greater advantages than the poor from the virtue and sense of duty of the rich. Further, that body of men forms, by their learning, the indispensable safeguard of Christianity itself.

A religious national establishment is therefore a matter of national obligation. It is essential to the state, and is the foundation of the whole constitution, with which, and with every part of which, it holds an indissoluble union. Church and State are, in a constitutional point of view, inseparable ideas, and the principle runs through the whole system of the national polity. The English nation has never thought it wise to entrust that great fundamental interest of the whole to what they trust no part of their civil or military service; that is, to the unsteady and precarious contributions of individuals.*

SIR JAMES MACKINTOSH.

(1766—1832)

It is scarcely necessary to say that the principles set forth in the preceding pages are those on which our own constitutional system has been defended and maintained up to the present day. It has stood the assaults of all the shallow theories that have been brought to bear against it, for it has had on its side all that is greatest, wisest, and most eminent among the writers, orators, and statesmen of our country. No authority, I believe, could be quoted in support of this assertion which would carry more weight with

---

* Reflections on the Revolution in France; Burke's Works, Vol. ii, pp. 370—376.

it than that of the late Sir James Mackintosh, filled as he was with an ardent love of rational liberty, and gifted with "the most Baconian mind since Bacon."* In his admirable Discourse on the Law of Nature and Nations,—after stigmatizing those theories of government, such as that of Locke, "resting upon supposed compacts, which are altogether chimerical, which must be admitted to be false in fact, which, if they are considered as fictions, will be found to serve no purpose of just reasoning, and to be equally the foundation of a system of universal despotism in Hobbes, and of universal anarchy in Rousseau,"—he proceeds to say that, in the "unmixed forms of government, as the right of legislation is vested in one individual or in one order, it is obvious that the legislative power may shake off all the restraints which the laws have imposed on it. All such governments, therefore, tend towards despotism, and the securities which they admit against misgovernment are extremely feeble and precarious." He then states what is, in his opinion, the best form of government.

"The best security which human wisdom can devise seems to be the distribution of political authority among different individuals and bodies, with separate interests, and separate characters, corresponding to the variety of classes of which civil society is composed, each interested to guard their

---

* Macaulay.

own order from oppression by the rest; each also interested to prevent any of the others from seizing an exclusive, and therefore despotic power; and all having a common interest to co-operate in carrying on the ordinary and necessary administration of government." Such are our own institutions;— affording to all, according to his own admirable definition of true liberty, "protection against wrong both from their rulers and their fellows;" allowing all classes and conditions of men to be "undisturbed in the exercise of their natural powers;" offering the freest opportunity for the full development of the powers and capacities of each. " Such governments," he adds, "are, with justice, peculiarly and emphatically called *free;* and in ascribing that liberty to the skilful combination of mutual dependence and mutual check, I feel my own conviction greatly strengthened, by calling to mind, that in this opinion I agree with all the wise men who have ever deeply considered the principles of politics—with Aristotle and Polybius, with Cicero and Tacitus, with Bacon and Machiavel, with Montesquieu and Hume."* To this he subjoins in a note: " To the weight of these great names let me add the opinion of two illustrious men of the present age, as both their opinions are combined by one of them in the following passage. In his speech on the Army Estimates, 9th February, 1790, Mr. Fox

---

* Mackintosh's Discourse on the Law of Nature and Nations. London, 1800, pp. 46—51.

said he always thought any of the simple unbalanced governments bad—simple monarchy, simple aristocracy, simple democracy: he held them all imperfect or vicious; all were bad by themselves; the composition alone was good. These had been always his principles, in which he agreed with his friend Mr. Burke."

As to the origin of government, to discover which Locke, and after him Rousseau, in his Contrat Social, employed their speculations, Sir James Mackintosh remarks that such speculations are scarcely worthy of serious notice; that the origin of government rested not on any supposed contract, but upon the solid basis of general convenience. Men cannot subsist without society and mutual aid; the protection of government is necessary to them; to enjoy that protection they must submit to restraints; thence the duty of obedience, and the reciprocal duties of magistrates; an argument "which directly and fully answers the only rational end for which the fiction of a contract could have been invented."

He then closes the argument with this noble passage. "I shall not encumber my reasoning by any speculations on the origin of government, a question upon which so much reason has been wasted in modern times, but which the ancients, in a higher spirit of philosophy, never once deigned to stir. If our principles be just, the origin of government must have been coeval with that of mankind, and as no tribe has ever yet been discovered so brutish as to be without some government, and yet so enlightened as to establish a government by common consent, it is surely unnecessary to employ any serious argument in the confutation of a doctrine inconsistent with reason, and wholly unsupported by experience."[*]

He refers in a note to the fact that this argument is as old as Aristotle "who, in the Introduction to the First Book of his 'Politics,' demonstrated the necessity of political society to the well-being, and indeed the very existence of man" (see above, pp. 1—5), and that "the same scheme of philosophy is admirably pursued by Polybius, in the short but invaluable fragment of the Sixth Book of his History." (See above, p. 82.)

EARL RUSSELL. | JOHN STUART MILL.

The principles thus shown to have recommended themselves to the highest reason of many successive generations were taken as the basis of the great measures for the Reform of Parliament in 1832 and 1867.

The time is approaching when another change in the same direction will be made, by the extension of the borough franchise to the counties.

---

[*] Mackintosh's Discourse on the Law of Nature and Nations London, 1800, pp. 46, 47.

The problem will then be, how to make this great addition to the voting power of the country without disturbing the relative position of the respective members of the body politic.

The mode of solving this problem—namely, by the representation of minorities—was submitted to parliament by Lord John Russell, in his Bill for the Amendment of the Representation, in 1854, in the following words:—

"Very great advantage would be derived from a change which has been advocated in writing and in pamphlets, and which was suggested by my noble friend, Lord Grey, in a public document, emanating from a Committee of the Privy Council; namely, that a representation should be given to the minority. Sometimes, in the larger counties and cities, 2,000, 3,000, or 4,000 voters who voted for an unsuccessful candidate experience great soreness and irritation at their perpetual exclusion from the representation. The more you have your representation confined to large populations, the more you ought to take care that there should be some kind of balance. . . . . When there is a large body excluded it cannot be said that the community is fairly represented." (Hansard, Vol. 130, p. 496, Feb. 13th, 1854.)*

In his work on the English Constitution and

---

* One of the pamphlets referred to was doubtless that by Mr. James Garth Marshall, on Minorities and Majorities; their relative Rights. A Letter to Lord John Russell. London, 1853.

Government, in 1865, Lord John Russell, then become Earl Russell, sets forth the principle more fully. Arguing against the vague fears, that by a large extension of the suffrage the working classes would by their numbers swallow up all other classes, Earl Russell gives it as his opinion that "this apprehension may be removed by a judicious modification of the proposed suffrage, and by a happy sense on the part of the public, that an addition of the votes of the most intelligent of the working classes to the constituent body will form a security and not a danger." (Page 4.) And while objecting to the suggestions for giving a plurality of votes to property, and to Mr. Thomas Hare's peculiar scheme for securing the representation of minorities, by allowing voters in any part of the kingdom to vote for particular candidates, as contrivances altogether unknown to our habits, Earl Russell proceeds to say, that "If there were to be any deviation from our customary habits and rooted ideas on the subject of representation, I should like to see such a change as I once proposed, in order to obtain representation of the minority in large and populous counties and towns. If, when three members are to be chosen, an elector were allowed to give two votes to one candidate, we might have a Liberal county gentleman sitting for Buckinghamshire, and a Conservative manufacturer for Manchester. The local majority would have two to one in the House of Commons, and the minority would not feel itself disfranchised and degraded. Yet even this change would be difficult to introduce, and would perhaps be unpalatable in its first working." (Ibid., p. 4.)*

Mr. John Stuart Mill, in 1861, expressed his approval of the same idea in his Considerations on Representative Government, p. 138. "Lord John Russell, in one of his reform bills, introduced a provision that certain constituencies should return three members, and that in these each elector should be allowed to vote only for two. Thus a minority equal to or exceeding a third would be able to return one member." And in pp. 131—148 he gives his reasons for that approval.

"The dangers that beset a representative democracy are," he says, "two; 1st, a low grade of intelligence in the representative body, and 2nd, class legislation by the numerical majority. . . By our present representative system the electors who are on a different side from the local majority are unrepresented. . . . This virtual blotting out of the minority is no necessary or natural consequence of freedom, although until recently it was thought to be so by all the friends of freedom. It is diametrically opposed to the first principles of democracy—representation in proportion to numbers. It is an essential principle of democracy that minorities should be adequately represented. No real democracy, nothing but a false show of democracy

---

* The original proposal, that in constituencies returning three members every elector should have only two votes, has been attributed to Mr. Winthrop Mackworth Praed, M.P., in 1831. (Hansard, Vol. 188, p. 1075.)

is possible without it." . . . "The tendency of representative government is towards collective mediocrity. This tendency is increased by every reduction and extension of the franchise. The voice of the instructed minority may have no organs at all in the representative body. . . . The conflict of opinion is necessary to healthy existence; the absence of it would produce stagnation and decay." (Page 148.)

. . "The representative system ought to be so constituted as not to allow any of the various sectional interests to be so powerful as to be capable of prevailing against truth and justice, and the other sectional interests combined." (Page 129.)

In his previous volume of Dissertations, Political, Philosophical, and Historical (1859), Mill—arguing strongly against Bentham's political principles which would, equally with Locke's, lead to "the despotism of the opinion of the majority told by the head," and also, as he has said of Locke's,* would prove that representative democracy was equally applicable for Bedouins and Malays—thus expressed himself (p. 379) :—

"The numerical majority of any society whatever must consist of persons all standing in the same social position, and having in the main the same pursuits, namely, unskilled manual labourers, and we mean no disparagement to them; whatever we say to their disadvantage we say equally to that of the numerical majority of shopkeepers or of squires. Where there

---

* Considerations on Representative Government, p. 36.

is identity of position and pursuits there also will be identity of partialities, passions, and prejudices; and to give to one set of partialities, passions, and prejudices absolute power, without counterbalance from other partialities, passions, and prejudices of a different sort, is the way to make those imperfections hopeless; to make one narrow, mean type of human nature universal and perpetual; and to crush the influence which tends to the further improvement of man's intellectual and moral nature." (Page 380.)

Mr. J. G. Marshall thus gives the results of his experience at page 25 of his pamphlet above mentioned:

"In many localities the minorities are habitually swamped and voiceless; numbers would show a very respectable but a silenced minority. Indirect palliatives of this mischief (such as, among others, the virtual representation of those minorities elsewhere) are not sufficient; all would leave a great weight of inequality and injustice. Minorities so swamped either constantly labour under a sore feeling of injustice and oppression, abandon all attempts at choice in exercising their political rights, or resort to fraudulent means and corruption. The majority have a monopoly of power, and being without wholesome restraint become tyrannical and bigoted. Can it be seriously argued that to balance one great mischief against another is as wise and safe a mode of proceeding as to endeavour to avoid both?"

The same view is taken by the writer of an article in the *Edinburgh Review* on the Representation of

Minorities (July, 1854), who adopts the opinion that "the minority in every large county and borough should have a fair share in the representation; that a national assembly should be a reflex as much as it can be rendered of the nation itself; and that all such elections should be so conducted that every voter should be put into a position to exercise an intelligent choice. The principle of providing for a representation of the minority is one which will one day be seen to be indispensable to any system of real representation. If the House of Commons is to be the mainspring of our government, and to retain its political and moral ascendancy, it ought to contain in its ranks the leading men of all opinions. We should regard it as a misfortune if able and fair men belonging to all parties in the state were not present at its discussions."

Sir G. Cornewall Lewis, in his Dialogue on the Best Form of Government (1863), while acknowledging that the decision of the majority is necessary for the purpose of government; that on the whole it had worked well; and that in this country the dominant majorities are accustomed to abstain from the extreme use of their superior power; nevertheless grounded his approval on the fact of the existence in his time of small constituencies through which "the interests and arguments of minorities had found a voice." "By a proper application," he says, "of the method of local representation, and by the formation of limited constituencies, the representation of minorities can be legitimately accomplished." It is obvious, therefore, that in proportion as limited constituencies disappear, a fair field must be provided for the exposition of the interests and arguments of minorities, by means of a new and effectual method of local representation.

To the same effect also was the opinion of the late Mr. Walter Bagehot, than whom no modern political writer was entitled to higher respect. At page 345 of his work On the English Constitution (London, 1867), he quotes from a pamphlet written by himself in 1859 as follows:—

> "We would give each of the great cities with low suffrage three members, and allow all the voters to give their votes to one member. This would give the rich and cultivated one member at least; for they would always be a large minority, and any minority greater than a fourth is by this plan sure of a seat."

The principle thus advocated by Mr. Bagehot was proposed in a different form by Mr. Lowe during the discussions on the Reform of the Representation in 1867. On the 4th July of that year Mr. Lowe moved that "Where there are more than two members, and more than one seat is vacant, every voter shall be entitled to a number of votes equal to the number of vacant seats, and may give all such votes to one candidate, or may distribute them among the candidates as he may think fit." (Hansard, Vol. 188, p. 1038.) But this proposition of the "cumulative vote" was strongly opposed, more especially as it was to be applied to the whole kingdom, and therefore went further than the alleged need; and it was negatived by a majority of 141.

But when the bill reached the House of Lords the more moderate remedy—to which public attention had, during so many years, been called by Earl Russell and Mr. Mill and other authorities—by which, in a definite number of constituencies having three members, each elector should be allowed to vote for two only, was proposed as an amendment by Earl Cairns, strongly supported by Earl Russell; and notwithstanding the opposition of the Conservative ministry was, by a union of Liberal and Conservative votes, added to the bill; the numbers voting being Contents 142, Non-contents 51; majority 91.

When brought down to the House of Commons, this amendment was warmly contested by some of the leading members of the Liberal party and by the government, but was carried by a similar non-party vote; the numbers for its rejection being Ayes 204, Noes 253; majority for accepting it, 49.

The discussion in both Houses on Earl Cairns' amendment is, I believe, fairly represented by the following summary.

Against it the arguments were that—

The large boroughs are great centres of political life; their majorities lead the political opinion of the country.

The fair weight they are entitled to would be diminished by giving a representative to the minority.

The principle is new; it recognises numbers instead of communities, and points to electoral districts.

Communities have hitherto been considered an integral part of the constitution.

The practice of the constitution has always been that the majority of voices has elected the members.

To enable a minority to elect a representative would impair the influence of the constituent body looked upon as a whole.

The minority vote would neutralize one of the majority; thus taking away half of its voting power in the House of Commons.

To give a vote to the minority would be to deaden political life in the constituencies.

By preventing contests the constituencies would lose all the instruction that contests afford.

The members elected by the majority are bound to look to the welfare and interests of the whole.

The minority would seek the means of being represented in other quarters.

There would be injustice in the limited and partial application of the principle.

It would also be rendered illusory at every bye election, when the majority would resume their power.

So many bye elections occur during each long parliament, that the action of the minority vote might affect the power of a party, while there was no change of opinion in the country generally.

The member for a minority would be a delegate.

There had been no sufficient time given for the discussion of this new principle.

In favour of Earl Cairns' amendment the arguments were that—

If the numbers of the majorities in the great constituencies are so large as to tell with great weight, the minorities are also large, and are entitled to a distinct voice.

The majorities claim now more than their fair weight, as on many great subjects, local and general, they do not speak the opinions of a large minority.

Any plan for the representation of minorities must operate in a very great degree to diminish and control the tyranny of majorities.

The principle, undoubtedly, is new, but so also is the great extension given to the franchise. Innovations are familiar to the constitution. One innovation makes another needful, to counteract it.*

---

* "The greatest innovation that could be introduced into the Constitution of England would be a vote that there could be no innovation

Although to grant representation to a minority is a "homage to numbers," it is not more so than the giving a third member to large constituencies.

It is a fallacy to consider the constituency and the majority of the constituency the same thing.°

The majority of a large constituency cannot be adequately represented by a prominent member of it being returned for a small constituency elsewhere. Such a member could not speak with the same authority on subjects affecting his own locality. The minority is not less local because it is a minority.†

With the extension of the franchise the number of small constituencies must be reduced. Many more small boroughs must be grouped together. More large constituencies must be formed.

This must lead to uniformity of representation, and consequently to the loss of the mediating element which is now derived from the members not sent by either of the two great classes of the people—those of the county and the towns.

The minority vote would provide the variety required. If introduced in constituencies returning three members, the vote of the majority of those constituencies in the House of Commons would be still two to one.

It would foster political feeling among the minority, and to some extent supply the place of the small boroughs. It would not put an end to, but encourage contests, and the instruction they afford.

---

in it. The greatest beauty of the constitution was, that in its very principle it admitted of perpetual improvements which time and circumstances rendered necessary. It was a constitution, the chief excellence of which was that it admitted of perpetual reform." Speeches of the Right Hon. Charles James Fox. London, 1815, Vol. iv, p. 410.

* Burke recognises "local residence" as giving as full a title to united political action as "corporate capacity," and attributes to the petitions to parliament of a resident body an exceptional claim to be heard. (Vol. iii of Works, Edit. 1855, p. 499.) The principle applies to the claim of a large minority of residents to be directly heard by their representative.

† Burke was of opinion that virtual representation, in which he recognised a certain value, could not to any great extent supply the place of direct. "Virtual representation," he says, "is that in which there is a communion of interests, and a sympathy in feelings and desires, between those who act in the name of any description of people, and the people in whose name they act." . . . . "But this sort of virtual representation cannot have a long or sure existence, if it has not a substratum in the actual. The member must have some relation to the constituent." (Vol. iii, pp. 334, 335.) When representing one place, a member cannot be said to be acting in the name of another.

In constituencies where one party holds irresistible sway the minority become apathetic, and political life is extinguished. The intelligence and property of the minority may feel itself misrepresented on many great subjects, yet without redress.

If there was a fair representation of minorities in a certain number of the large constituencies, a further extension of the franchise might be made with safety.

If we follow democratic countries in widely extending the suffrage, we should avoid their error of excluding the cultivated classes.

"The art of representation, like other arts, is progressive. The representation of minorities is an advance in the science of government."

If the arguments in favour of granting representation to the minority, in a limited number of large constituencies in counties and in towns, prevailed in the discussions on the Reform of the Representation in 1867, by a non-party vote in both Houses of Parliament, they may be expected to tell with even greater force in the deliberations that will before long occupy the public mind on the subject of extending the borough franchise to the counties.

This subject was again brought before the public in 1879. In the number of the *Nineteenth Century* for August in that year it was fully discussed by Mr. Leonard Courtney, M.P., late Under-Secretary of State for the Home Department, now Under-Secretary of State for the Colonies. Mr. Courtney argues that the present system of the representation of majorities acts unjustly to the constituencies and to the detriment of the representative body. He affirms that if the principle of the representation also of the minorities were adopted in large constituencies, this important result would be assured—namely, "the security that in the body elected there will be an accurate reflection of the persons who elected them." Under the present system the large body composing the minority in such constituencies has no living connection with the governing body of the country. It has no certainty that its interests will not be overlooked. "No party can be trusted to do justice to an excluded party. No one possesses the intelligence and imagination necessary before he can put himself in the position of another, so as to understand what the other wants.".... "There is no connection between the excluded minority and the ruling majority. If men obtain no share in the representation which constitutes the authority of a country, their political energies die away and disappear." On the other hand, if the large minorities were duly represented, "there would be a Chamber of larger information, of broader sympathies, and of wider aim than any we can now possess." Mr. Courtney adds, "We are so accustomed to the system we have, that we call it natural, although it is in the highest degree artificial; and we are disposed to reject as artificial what is in truth most simple and natural." (Pages 144—152.)

Burke has thus expressed the same principle. "We are so little affected by things that are habitual, that we consider the idea of the decision of the majority as if it were a law of our original nature. But such constructive whole, residing in a part only, is one of the most violent fictions of positive law that ever has been or can be made on the principles of artificial incorporation. Out of civil society, nature knows nothing of it; nor are men, even when arranged according to civil order, otherwise than by very long training, brought to submit to it at all. The mind is brought far more easily to acquiesce in the proceedings of one man."*

The principle of "electoral districts," each containing an approximately equal number of electors, and each district returning one member, which has been adopted in some countries, is shown by Mr. Courtney to be still more liable to lead to the total exclusion of the minority, and he illustrates what might take place frequently under that system by what actually occurred in Lancashire and in Birmingham. "In Lancashire, in 1868, there were 22 Conservative members elected against 11 Liberals; and yet, while 104,000 votes were given for Liberal members, only 102,000 votes were given to the Conservatives." In this case the distribution of voters favoured the Conservative minority, and gave them twice the number of members obtained by the Liberals. From the opposite point of view also, had Lancashire been formed into one great district, the large minority of 102,000 voters would have been without a representative. In Birmingham, on the other hand, in the election for the town council, the Liberals being a majority in each ward into which the town is divided, all the members of the town council in the

---

* Appeal from the New to the Old Whigs, 1791, p. 82.

year in which Mr. Courtney wrote (1879) were, with one doubtful exception, Liberals. In such cases, Mr. Courtney says, "We run the risk of injustice being ignorantly done to the unrepresented; we condemn to atrophy and extinction the political energies of the minority; we throw away the use of such practical talents as they may possess, and, after all, we cannot be sure that we obtain, upon a division of opinion in the town council, a reflex of the division of opinion among the electorate on the same question." (Pages 146—148.)*

---

* In connection with this subject, it has been noticed that the necessity of obliging members undertaking high office to undergo re-election will call for reconsideration.

In the Reform Bill, 1854, which was ultimately withdrawn, Lord John Russell introduced a clause proposing that the Statute of the 6th Anne (c. 7, s. 26)—requiring that if any person, being chosen member of the House of Commons, shall accept an office of profit from the crown, his election shall be void, but that he should be capable of re-election—should be repealed, and that the acceptance of office under the crown should be allowed without re-election, as in the reign of William III. (Hansard, Vol. 130, p. 496.)

On the 2nd of August, 1867, Earl Grey proposed in the House of Lords, as an amendment to the bill of that year, for the further amending the Representation of the People, "That no member of the House of Commons should vacate his seat by the acceptance of an office which does not disqualify him from sitting in Parliament if re-elected." It was argued that the present practice limited the choice of men to fill high offices; that it was essential that there should be no check upon the power of the crown to fill the high offices of State; that the practice was inconsistent, as it did not apply to the important offices of secretaries of the Treasury and Admiralty, or to the under-secretaries of the Home Office, the Colonies, or the India Office, and that there was no longer any fear of the undue influence of the crown, which gave rise to the enactment of the 6th Anne. (Hansard, Vol. 189, p. 793.)

The proposition was accepted in a modified form, by the 52nd Clause of the Act of 1867, which enacts that members already in office, accepting other offices, shall not vacate their seats.

The former jealousy of the powers of the crown in reference to appointments to office having ceased to exist, the probability that the

Some authorities have thought that the representation might be improved by two other methods; the first, by adding to the localities having only one member; the second, by dividing constituencies into wards, one or two of which would presumably consist of the upper classes, and the rest chiefly of the manual labour class. Both plans are open to grave objection. Under the first, the tendency would be to condemn one party to a perpetual minority; the second would encourage the separation of classes, and the representation of class interests, while affording to minorities no better opportunity of obtaining a voice in the legislature.

On the great principles of government, as applicable to this kingdom, John Stuart Mill and Earl Russell are also at one. The opinions of each may be thus summarised.

In his Considerations on Representative Government (1861, pp. 11—152), Mill insists, that to inquire into the best mode of government in the abstract (as it is called) is not a chimerical, but a highly practical employment of scientific intelligence. And to determine what kind of government is suited to this or

---

interests of a constituency would suffer by its member accepting office being very small, and the embarrassment to public businesss arising from the present practice being often very great, it will doubtless be found expedient to review this question in connection with that of any further adoption of the minority seats in the larger constituencies. Where these minority seats are created, one of their principal objects—the stability of the seat—would be frustrated if, immediately after a general election involving a change of government, the holder of one of those seats should, on accepting office, be sent back to the constituent body, with the certainty of being rejected by the majority.

that state of society, we must borrow from political philosophy its general principles.

He then passes in review the Italian republics, the free towns of Flanders and of Germany, the French democracy, the United States, and the States of South America, and compares their modes of government and their results with our own, taking his illustrations and enforcing his arguments equally from the examples of Greek history and from the practices he had observed in his own day in Marylebone, Finsbury, and Lambeth; thus manifesting his assent to the maxim, that the actions and passions of men under similar circumstances, whether on a large or a small scale, have been, and will continue to be, alike in all ages.

Acknowledging his preference for the mixed form of government, to which a certain balance of power is necessary, he observes that "that there is almost always a balance, but the scales never hang exactly even" (p. 87). But if one of the three powers should in this country threaten to overbear the others, it may be expected that the latter will unite to prevent it. The positive political morality of the country is the safeguard against allowing one of the three forces to dominate over the others." It is the business of the statesman to devise the means by which this result may be secured.

But instead of aiming at ascendancy, "A democracy," in Mill's opinion, "has enough to do in providing itself with an amount of mental competency sufficient for its own proper work, that of superintendence and check." (Ibid.)

How is it to obtain this? It depends, he says, on the proper constitution of the representative body. " In proportion as in its composition it fails to secure this amount of mental competency, it will endeavour to encroach on the province of the executive; . . . . it will countenance or impose a selfish, a capricious, an impetuous, or a short-sighted, ignorant, and prejudiced general policy, foreign and domestic." . . "The universal tradition, grounded on universal experience, is of the liability of men to be corrupted by power."

It should be the aim of a democracy "to get leaders of a higher grade of intelligence than themselves." Under the influence of "superior and guiding minds," they may be proof against demagogic artifices, which may aim at class ascendancy; and they may, on the other hand, acquire a true public spirit, in which is implied a disinterested regard for others, for the idea of posterity, of their country, and of mankind. A certain amount of conscience, of disinterested public spirit, may be fairly calculated upon in the citizen of any community ripe for representative government. This would be cultivated and enlarged in proportion as public questions and the principles of government became a more general object of serious study.

In his volume of Dissertations and Discussions, Political, Philosophical, and Historical" (1859), Mill represents, with great fairness, the unsoundness of the political reasoning by which Locke led the way to the pure democracies of modern times, and Bentham lent to them his additional authority.

In his Dissertations on Bentham in that volume (p. 379), he powerfully controverts his political principles, and gives an estimate of his merits and defects as a thinker and writer, of which the following is a brief reproduction.

Bentham's most important field of reform was that of practical abuses, especially those of his own profession—the law. All the great improvements both in the science and practice of law which have been in progress since his time are traceable to his influence.

His method of inquiry also—the application of the inductive philosophy to ethics,—introduced into morals and politics those habits of thought and modes of investigation which are essential to the idea of science. "It was not his opinions, but his method, that constituted the value of what he did; a value beyond all price, even if we should reject the whole, as we unquestionably must a large part, of the opinions themselves." . . . "This method was a security for accuracy, but not for comprehensiveness." . . . "Bentham failed in deriving light from other minds. He had neither internal experience nor external. The quiet tenour of his life conspired to exclude him from both. Other ages and nations were a blank to him for the purpose of instruction." . . . "No one probably, who, in a highly-instructed age, attempted to give a rule to human conduct, set out with a more limited conception either of the agencies by which human conduct is, or of those by which it should be influenced." (Pages 332—356.)

Man, as conceived by Bentham, is a being susceptible of pleasure and pain. His impelling and restraining principles consist, according to him, only of self-love and hatred. The world is considered by him as a collection of persons pursuing each his separate pleasure or interest; "each prevented from jostling the other by the fear of the penalties of the law, or the expectation of the pains or pleasures arising from the favour or disfavour of his fellow-creatures or of the Ruler of the Universe. There is an entire absence of recognition of conscience as distinct from philanthropy, or from affection to God or man, or from self-interest in this world or the next." . . . " The words rectitude, moral duty, self-respect, never occur; honour, love of beauty, or of power, or of order, are not recognised as springs of action." (Pages 354, 355.)

A theory of government proceeding from a mind constituted as was Bentham's was not likely to be complete. Promulgated at a time of reaction against the aristocratic governments of Modern Europe which were founded on the entire sacrifice of the community to the self-interest and ease of the few, his theory found favour with the vast numbers whose sympathies were excited on behalf of the sufferers by the abuses of those governments. "Not content with enthroning the majority as sovereign by means of universal suffrage, without king or House of Lords, he exhausted all the resources of ingenuity in devising the means of rivetting the yoke of public opinion closer and closer round the necks of all public functionaries, and excluding every possibility of the exercise of the slightest or most temporary influence either of a minority, or by the functionary's own notion of right." . . . This was "to pass from one form of bad government to another." (Pages 379—381.)

As a security for good government "it is necessary," Mill says, "that the institutions of society should make provision for keeping up, in some form or another, as a corrective to partial views, and a shelter for freedom of thought and individuality of character, a perpetual and standing opposition to the will of the majority. All countries which have been continuously progressive, or been durably great, have been so because there has been an organized opposition to the ruling powers, of whatever kind that ruling power was." . . "Almost all the greatest men who ever lived have formed part of such an opposition." . . "A centre of resistance is as necessary when the opinion of the majority is sovereign, as when the ruling power is a hierarchy or an aristocracy."* . . . "Where no such *point d'appui* exists there the human race will inevitably degenerate, and the question whether the United States, for instance, will in time sink into another China (also

---

* Burke has said that "Difficulty is a severe instructor. He that wrestles with us strengthens our nerves and sharpens our skill. Our antagonist is our helper. This amicable conflict with difficulty obliges us to an intimate acquaintance with our object, and compels us to consider it in all its relations. It will not suffer us to be superficial." (Works, Vol. ii, p. 487. Edit. 1855.)

a most commercial and industrious nation), resolves itself to us into the question, whether such a centre of resistance will gradually evolve itself or not." (P. 380.)

" Surely," he adds, " when any power has been made the strongest, enough has been done for it; care is thenceforward wanted rather to prevent that strongest power from swallowing up all others. Whenever all the forces of society act in one single direction, the just claims of the individual human being are in extreme peril. The power of the majority is salutary so far as it is used defensively;—as its exercise is tempered by respect for the personality of the individual and deference to the superiority of cultivated intelligence." . . . "If Bentham had employed himself in pointing out the means by which institutions fundamentally democratic might be best adapted to the preservation and strengthening of these two sentiments, he would have done something more permanently valuable and more worthy of his great intellect." (Page 381.)

"The bad part of Bentham's writings," in Mill's opinion, "is his resolute denial of that which he does not see. He thereby encouraged others to deny or disparage all feelings and mental states of which they have no consciousness themselves." . . . "A thoughtful regard for previous thinkers, and for the collective mind of the human race, is a necessary part of the philosophical character. There he will find the remainder of the truth of which he sees but half." (Pages 356—358.)

OMNIPOTENCE OF THE MAJORITY.

The course of thought which suggested itself to Mill, in 1859 and 1861, on the action of pure democracies, had already, in 1835, led De Tocqueville to the same conclusions. from his personal observations in the United States. He calls attention, in his chapter on the " Omnipotence of the Majority,"* to the fact that " it is the individual States that really direct American society," and that the change that had begun in many of them, in the mode of electing their representatives, and in electing them for very short terms, had artificially added to the natural power of the majority. The consequences had already begun to develop themselves; the instability of legislation had become very great, from the constant change of representatives, and there was no country in the world in which laws had such short duration. In many of the States the independence of the judges had been destroyed by their being elected by the people, and for short periods, and the representatives were so strictly tied down to certain instructions, as to be converted into mere delegates. The changes noted by De Tocqueville as having then begun, have been since extended to the whole of the individual States. I have therefore thought it desirable, as already mentioned (p. 138), to describe them in an appendix,† setting forth their origin and tracing their progress to the present time.

---

* De la Démocratie en Amerique, par Alexis de Tocqueville. Paris, 1835, Vol. iii, ch. 7.
† Appendix B.

De Tocqueville pronounced the consequences of these great social and political changes to be "disastrous, and dangerous for the future." He asserted that they put in peril true liberty, "by making one social power supreme, with no obstacle to restrain its steps and afford it time for consideration." He remarked that it had already produced an injurious effect on the national character. "When the American revolution broke out, a crowd of remarkable men appeared in public life, and if the opinion of the day had its influence on their minds, it did not tyrannise over them. The celebrated men of that epoch, taking their full part in the public movement, had, nevertheless, a grandeur of their own; they spread their fame over the nation, and did not borrow it from the position in which the nation had placed them." . . . . "The independence of thought which marks great characters was becoming rare." . . . . The tyranny of an absolute government strikes the body, but the mind is beyond its reach. The tyranny of a majority lets the body go free, but aims directly at the mind ("*va droit à l'âme*"). "If ever liberty is lost in America, the fault will be with the omnipotence of the majority in driving the minority to despair, and causing them to appeal to material force." Referring, in confirmation of his conclusions, to a letter of Jefferson's to Madison, De Tocqueville says: "I prefer to cite Jefferson in preference to anyone else, because I consider him the most powerful apostle that democracy has ever had." Jefferson said, in that letter

(15th August, 1789): " The executive power in our government is not the only, it is not perhaps the principal object of my solicitude. The tyranny of the members of the legislatures is at this moment, and will be for many years to come, the danger most to be feared. The tyranny of the executive power will arrive in its turn, but after a more remote period."

EARL RUSSELL ON REPRESENTATION.

Earl Russell, in his book on the English Constitution and Government (1865—1873), equally combats the doctrines of Locke and Bentham, that every man of sound mind and years of discretion has an unalienable right to vote belonging to him, as a member of a free country, thus including the whole adult male population. This proposition takes no account of the end to be obtained. The purpose in view is good government, the freedom and welfare of the whole people within the state, and their security from without. The problem is the best mode of attaining this end. " A representation that should produce hasty, passionate, unjust, and ignorant decisions, could not conduce to the welfare of the people, which is the supreme law."

" If it is said" (as it is by Locke) "that no part of the property of the people ought to be levied in taxes by the Government, without the consent expressed or implied of the whole community, it might be answered that a man's life and liberty are as valuable to him as his property, yet no one contends that the judicial body, and the jury in criminal cases, should be elected by universal suffrage."

But the suffrage being a means to an end, and that end being the freedom and welfare of the whole community, it becomes a matter of expediency on whom it should be conferred. "The mighty power of selecting the House of Commons should be entrusted to a portion of the community, qualified by honesty and intelligence." . . . "The suffrage should be attainable by industry and thrift, like the old forty-shilling freehold, or the payment of scot and lot in the boroughs. That is quite as philosophical a basis of representation as the metaphysical categories of modern times." (Page 224.)

Earl Russell points out that the old franchises of the forty-shilling freeholders, and the payment of scot and lot in boroughs, implied the following qualifications: 1st. The possession of an average amount of intelligence. 2nd. A security for the stability of property. 3rd. A probable exemption from the taint of corruption. 4th. A condition of life which identified the voter with the general sense of the community—in short, with the public opinion of his time.

In addition to the qualification of the voter there is necessary, to attain the end in view, a proper distribution of seats. Otherwise, "in large cities population would outweigh property, and in large counties, property would outweigh population." It has been already shown how Earl Russell proposed to provide for this necessity, partly by grouping together some of the smaller boroughs, partly by securing in large constituencies the representation of minorities, and that with the impending further extension of the franchise and grouping of boroughs, the representation of minorities, partially introduced in 1867, will require also to be considerably extended. It will be by this alone that it will be possible, in large constituencies, to preserve the balance between population and property, and to insure that the representative body on the whole should present " a true image of the property and experience, the knowledge, and the wisdom of England."

Whatever may be the expectations of the advocates of pure democracy, Earl Russell felt it "hard to believe, in this age of the world, that there are any models of government still untried, promising a cup of felicity and of freedom which England has not tasted." . . . "The limit," he says, " appears to me to have been rightly laid down by the first Earl Grey. That which tends to increase the security of the prerogatives of the crown, the authority of both houses of parliament, and the rights and liberties of the people, may well be accepted; the plan, which has other objects, and looks to a different form of government, ought to be rejected." . . .
" Let it not be forgotten that the intolerance of a

despotism and of a democracy are alike unknown in the temperate zone of our ancient form of government."

To the same effect are the words of Sir Edward Creasy, in his Rise and Progress of the English Constitution (p. 398):—

"Our constitution must from time to time require remedial changes, and at present the anomalies of the distribution of the suffrage, and the shameful corruption with which its exercise is too often accompanied, are pressing upon our statesmen's anxious attention. He who has studied our constitution most deeply, will venerate it the most, and while he vigorously extirpates abuses, and steadily works out its vital law of growth and development, he will religiously guard its primary institutions from the experiments of the conceited theorist, and the assaults of the disloyal destroyer."

> "Love thou thy land, with love far-brought
> From out the storied Past, and used
> Within the Present, but transfused
> Thro' future time by power of thought."
>
> *   *   *   *   *   *   *
>
> "Make knowledge circle with the winds;
> But let her herald, Reverence, fly.
> Before her to whatever sky
> Bear seed of men and growth of minds."
>
> TENNYSON.

Postscript.—Sir James Mackintosh, in his valuable work, A Discourse on the Law of Nature and Nations, adverts to the fact that "the fashion of depreciating authority" and "attempting to philosophise without regard to fact and experience—the sole foundation of all true philosophy"—originated with the revolutionary writers of the French school. He intimates that his own practice in the pursuit of truth was to follow reason, supported by authority. It is " in the works of the great historians and philosophers of ancient and modern times" that he finds stated "the substance, the object, and the result of all morals, and politics, and law." He looks to them (as he tells us the great master of the science of the law of nations—Grotius—did before him) " as witnesses, whose conspiring testimony, mightily strengthened and confirmed by their discordance on almost every other subject, is conclusive proof of the unanimity of the whole human race on the great rules of duty and the fundamental principles of morals." . . . . " Even Virtue and Wisdom themselves acquire," he says, " new majesty in my eyes when 1 thus see all the great masters of thinking and writing called together, as it were, from all times and countries, to do them homage and to appear in their train." (Pages 17, 20, 72.)

APPENDIX A.

(Referred to in Page 171.)

M. DE TOCQUEVILLE

AND OTHER AUTHORITIES

ON THE

"OLD GOVERNMENT OF FRANCE AND THE REVOLUTION."

The two great countries whose governments are now based on the principles of Locke and Rousseau—France and the United States—cannot be said to give proof of the superior results anticipated from those principles.

With regard to France, her best friends lament the instability that, for nearly a hundred years, has followed the overthrow of all authority resting on the ancient foundations. M. de Tocqueville has amply proved[*] that it was reform, and not revolution, that should have been resorted to for correcting the abuses of the old government; and that the way to substantial and salutary reform was shown in the old representative assemblies that still existed in five of the

---

[*] L'Ancien Régime et la Révolution. Par Alexis de Tocqueville. Paris, 1856.

provinces and in some other small districts. Those of Bretagne and Languedoc were in full vigour. The assemblies were composed of representatives of the clergy, the nobles, and the commonalty. That of Languedoc (comprising 2,000,000 inhabitants) was convoked annually; had free liberty of speech; raised all their own taxes, and a portion of those of the state, in their own manner, and executed all their own public works (p. 325). " With these examples before them, the modern spirit might have penetrated peaceably into these old institutions, and modified all, without destroying anything." (Page 340.)

The error committed in breaking entirely with the past, instead of reforming on the basis of the existing institutions and usages, has, M. de Tocqueville says, inflicted upon France wounds from which she will never recover. The error arose out of the political condition of the country. The extinction of liberty from the time when Richelieu (1624—1642) broke the power of the nobility and made France an absolute monarchy; the consequent absence, during all the succeeding generations, of a class of statesmen trained in political affairs, and of organised parties directing public opinion, left the Revolution, when it did break out, to be guided by speculative writers, according to abstract principles and general theories which they had themselves conceived. Consequently, instead of attacking separately bad laws, they waged war against the whole, and destroyed the entire fabric of the ancient society. (Pages 311—323.)

The same view was taken by the late Sir George Cornewall Lewis,* who, to his experience as a practical statesman, added the highest qualities of a political philosopher and writer. He pointed out that the attacks of the *French* philosophers were chiefly directed against the Church and Religion; that it was the *Swiss* Rousseau whose doctrines formed the political creed of the Revolution, and that the true cause of the Revolution was the badness of the old government, and the absence of men capable of seeing through and effectually opposing the shallow doctrines that brought it about. " Voltaire, although an enemy of many of the abuses of the Ancien Régime, was far from being a democrat, a leveller, or a communist. The same remark applies to most of the other French Philosophers of the Regency and of the reign of Louis XV. They had no intention of undermining and destroying the government of the country. Voltaire reprobated the old customary laws on account of their variety; he did not attack the general form of government. . . . If the old institutions had been allowed to thaw gradually . . . the world would have been saved all the bloodshed and spoliation of the Revolution, and the desolating wars of the Empire (p. 58); and "if the French had not so effectually exterminated the old aristocracy they would have incurred less danger of falling under a single master." (Page 78.)

---

* A Dialogue on the Best Form of Government. By the Right Honorable Sir George Cornewall Lewis, Bart., M.P. London, 1863, pp. 50—52, 78.

The inquiries of De Tocqueville and Sir Cornewall Lewis confirmed the opinions which Burke had formed by personal observation in France a few years previously to the Revolution.

Writing in 1790, Bnrke said that he "was no stranger to the faults and defects of the subverted government of France;" but it was "not true that it was so incapable or undeserving of reform that it was an absolute necessity that the whole fabric should be at once pulled down, and the area cleared for the erection of a theoretic, experimental edifice in its place. All France was of a different opinion in the beginning of the year 1789. The instructions to the representatives to the States-General, from every district in the kingdom, were filled with projects for the reformation of that government, without the remotest suggestion of a design to destroy it." . . . His inquiries and observations did not present to him any incorrigible vices of the noblesse, or clergy, or monarchy of France which could not be removed by a reform very short of abolition." . . . "M. Necker found that very moderate alterations in the incidence of taxation would have restored the finances."* If there had been the wisdom to recur to, and to improve upon the model of their ancient provincial states, "they had in them the example of those opposed and conflicting interests which interpose a salutary check to all precipitate resolutions which render deliberation

---

* Reflections on the Revolution in France, pp. 398—410, 389.

a matter not of choice but of necessity, and make all change a subject of compromise, which naturally begets moderation."* Unfortunately blind prejudices, and the absence of all practical experience in statesmanship, the fruit of years of absolute government, rendered a wise course of transition impossible. As a consequence of these defects, and "by following the false lights of presumptuous speculation, France bought undisguised calamities at a higher price than any nation has purchased the most unequivocal blessings.†

Very remarkable illustrations of the truth of these several opinions have been disclosed within the last few years by various works in France, founded on hitherto unpublished documents from the archives of the secret police and other similar sources.

The interesting volumes of M. Taine, on the Old Régime, The Revolution, and the Jacobin Conquest, throw many new and ghastly lights on that most terrible of national tragedies, and fully unveil the causes which have made "Contemporary France" what she is.‡ Commenting upon the political incapacity of the upper classes, the result of despotism and its debasing accompaniments, M. Taine says (in his second volume, p. 398) that the noblesse, abandoning

---

* Reflections on the Revolution in France, p. 309.
† Ibid., p. 311.
‡ Les Origines de la France Contemporaine. Par H. Taine. L'Ancien Régime, Second Edition, 8vo, 1876. La Révolution, Vol. i, 1878. La Conquête Jacobine, Vol. ii, Paris, 1881. The first two vols. have been translated by Mr. J. Durand, in 3 vols., London, 1881. See also a very comprehensive article upon the subject, in the number of the *Quarterly Review* for January, 1882.

the public interests and themselves, surrendered at the first summons; and the spectacle was seen of an immense population of subjects, without rights, submitting themselves to a small despotic oligarchy, that constituted itself the sovereign people. The actual number by which that oligarchy was supported in Paris, was estimated at one time as low as between 4,000 and 6,000 men, and never higher than 10,000, in a population of 700,000; and in all France they were believed never to have exceeded one-tenth of the whole body of electors. (Page 399.) The vast majority, without organisation, without mutual respect or confidence, oppressed by misplaced taxation, and impoverished by the intolerable exactions of the old feudal laws, with deeply-seated jealousies and hatreds raging in their midst, were at the mercy of the reckless few who erected themselves into guides and governors, and believed themselves capable of solving, without preparation or experience, immense and complicated problems which men of the highest capacity and of special acquirements approach with hesitation. (Vol. ii, p. 28.)

It was over a people in the state of mental, moral, material, and political depression above described, that the spirit of the great intellectual revival of the 18th century came to move, and to stir it to its inmost depths. No wonder that one of the manifestations of that spirit—an enthusiastic belief in the possible regeneration of mankind on some new principle—should have been eagerly received into every heart.

Let us recall to mind, from the most recent and most fully-instructed authority on those subjects—M. Taine—what that belief was, the results of which are so amply set forth in his second and third volumes. He thus expounds it in his volume on the Old Régime. (Pages 289—328.)

It was a belief in a totally new view of human nature, promulgated by Rousseau; the reflex of the extraordinary and discordant structure of his own mind. The fundamental principle of his reasonings is, in his own words, that man is a being naturally good, loving justice and order. Remove from him all the restraints that laws and customs have placed upon him, and which have moulded him to what he is—depraved and miserable—and his instincts and his conscience will make him not only virtuous, but happy (pp. 290—293). Therefore, all hitherto established institutions, moral, political, and social—property, family, church—have had no foundation either in reason or justice, and must be destroyed.* The only useful and creditable occupations

---

* Rousseau's principle, that as all previous governments rested on usurped authority they should be destroyed, however good they may have been, however slight the prospect of replacing them by a better, and however great the danger to the national well-being, should be contrasted with that laid down by Burke, as alone justifying a revolution. The contrast cannot be better expressed than in the words of Mr. John Morley, in his exhaustive work on Rousseau: "The greatest, widest, and loftiest exposition of the bearings of expediency on government and its conditions is to be found in the magnificent and immortal writings of Burke;" .... in whose view "the true opposite of Rousseau's principle is, the right and duty of throwing off any government which inflicts more disadvantages than it confers advantages." (Rousseau, by John Morley. 2 Vols. 8vo, Chapman & Hall, 1873. Vol. ii, pp. 186, 187.)

are those which supply the primitive wants of mankind. All that has been regarded as "the flower of human life"—literature, manners, elegance, luxury—all these, and the swarms that live upon them, are parasites, and only exist to the detriment of the primitive equality which is the great heirloom of the race. The first man who enclosed a piece of land by his industry, and called it his own, was a criminal against all the rest. What he presumes to call his property, which no one had a right to concede to him, was a theft; for the earth and its fruits belong to all (p. 297). All the clauses of the "Social Contract" reduce themselves to one; namely, the total abandonment of each individual, with all his rights, his powers and his goods, to the commonalty. The state, as regards its members, is master of all their goods by the "Social Contract." The possessors are only considered the temporary holders of what belongs to the public.* Instead of the physical and mental inequalities which nature has made among men, the social agreement substitutes a moral and legitimate equality, so that, although unequal in power and genius, they become equal by convention and right ("pouvant être inégaux en force et en génie, ils deviennent égaux par convention et de droit"); and for the enjoyment of this "moral and legitimate equality," the equalisation of property must also be aimed at, so that while all have something, no one must have too

---

* Du Contrat Social, ou Principes du Droit Politique. Par J. J. Rousseau. Paris, 1790, Liv. i, ch. 6.

much ("d'où il suit que l'état social n'est avantageux aux hommes qu'autant qu'ils ont tous quelque chose, et qu'aucun d'eux n'a rien de trop").* The present fabric of political society had its origin in some early and iniquitous contract between the powerful rich and their feeble dupes. . . . . The real social contract was made by an assembly of men, all meeting for the first time, without traditions, without obligations, without country, all born accomplished moralists and politicians, all equal, and intending to preserve their equality; determined to settle a form of government and elect a magistrate over them, yet to retain their claim to be the sovereign people. (Taine, pp. 300 —305.) In the name of the sovereignty of the people they withdraw from the government all authority, all prerogative, all stability, and all power. The people is the sovereign, and the government but its clerk; even less, its domestic servant. The moment the people give themselves representatives they are no longer free. There must be no representatives; there must be delegates, who can determine nothing without the leave of those who sent them; who are deprived of all independent thought and action (pp. 316, 317). An absolutism is thus established, more complete than that of a single despot. The state becomes everything, the individual nothing. The state substitutes itself for the individual in all its acts. Henceforward it is the public will that governs; that is, in theory, the

---

* Contrat Social, Liv. i, ch. 9, and Note.

arbitrary and unchangeable decision of the majority counted by the head, but in fact, the rigid arbitrary will of the assembly, the faction, or the one man, the master for the moment of the public power (p. 327).

M. Taine has devoted a hundred pages of his first volume, to bringing again fully into view these theories, as a matter of history, and to recalling and amplifying the refutations of them which their first promulgation called forth in an abundant stream during the two succeeding generations.

The socialistic portion of those theories has exhibited of late years the great power they have obtained over the minds of the ill-instructed classes both in France and Germany; accompanied and strengthened as they have been by the writings of that numerous French school which, drawing their inspirations from Hobbes, denied that there was any other base of morality than that of self-love; asserted that pleasure and pain are the only springs of moral action; that it is as impossible to love the right for the sake of the right, as it is to love the evil for the sake of the evil; that to obtain and to preserve happiness is the only instinct, the only right, the only duty. Whatever you do for others is done from the motive of calculated self-interest. Virtue is therefore only long-sighted egotism. Man has no other reason for doing good, than the fear of some harm being done to himself.*

---

* Hobbes' Leviathan; Helvetius de l'Esprit, passim. The doctrines of all the writers of these materialistic and atheistical schools are well summed up by M. Taine, in his first volume, pp. 282—301.

These new sources of promised happiness have produced, instead, fierce discontent. That feeling formed a strong element in the insurrections in Germany in 1848; and socialistic doctrines are still baffling the statesmanship of that country. In France in 1848, those doctrines were for a time triumphant; and in 1871, the French army, smarting from the failure to defend Paris against the Germans, had to retake it, after a protracted struggle, from the insurgent socialists, whose hostility was chiefly directed against the middle classes, and whose name will be for ever stained by the murder, in cold blood, of the Archbishop of Paris, and a large number of his helpless attendants.

Nor is that fierce discontent likely to be allayed, as long as the minds of large masses of men are penetrated with the material, sceptical, or atheistical doctrines, derived from the writers above referred to. In vain, hitherto, has the despairing cry of a thoughtful Frenchman, "Give us back our religion," (Rendez-nous nôtre religion), been echoed and re-echoed by many both in his own and other countries.

The political portion of those theories, wherever adopted, is too attractive to a certain class of minds to be easily brought to relax its hold. Its vitality is a tribute to its power of affecting the imagination, and ministering food to the "envious fever" of ill-directed aspirations. The introduction of the Caucus among ourselves is one of the latest lessons we are called upon to learn from pure democracy. (See pp. 243-5, 250-3.)

Unsound as is the "Social Contract" as a theory, it would be unjust not to recognise its effect in raising Europe from the political torpor then almost universal. It is thus spoken of by one whose sympathies are too wide not to do Rousseau full justice.

"The 'Social Contract' is worked out precisely in that fashion which, if it touches men at all, makes them into fanatics. . . . It is dogma that gives fervour to a sect. There are always large classes of men to whom any theory in the shape of a vigorously compact system is irresistibly fascinating, and to whom the qualifications of a proposition, or a limitation of a theoretic principle, is distressing or intolerable."* The premises being assumed, Rousseau's conclusions follow with irresistible logical precision; and the premises are too tempting to be canvassed by those whom passion or suffering indisposes to the scrutiny, even if their intelligence made them capable of it. The "Social Contract," therefore, was "the match that kindled revolutionary fire in generous breasts throughout Europe. It was the virile and patriotic energy thus evoked that saved France from partition, and European civilization from the crushing supremacy of powers even more dark and retrograde than the first French empire." † The abuses of those times have everywhere given way to mild governments, and to great and continuous efforts for the general good.

---

* Rousseau, by John Morley. Vol. ii, pp. 134, 135.
† Ibidem, pp. 188, 189.

But (through its interpreters in this and other countries) the " Social Contract " is still, and will long remain, a social and political peril. It would be well that one maxim of Rousseau's should not be overlooked,—That the right of voting imposes the duty of instruction in its exercise (Le droit de d'y voter suffit pour m'imposer le devoir de m'en instruire." Contrat Social, Liv. i, c. 1).

The destruction of the aristocracy of France, to which Sir Cornewall Lewis refers above (p. 213), had drawn forth from Burke, in a brilliant passage, an analysis of the mode of growth of a natural aristocracy, of which the titled aristocracy is only a part, and which is recruited from time to time from the professions and from commerce. He points out the place which such a body holds in the social order. "It is not a separate interest in the state, or separable from it. It is an essential integrant part of any large body rightly constituted." And men qualified in the manner he describes,—by education and experience,—" form in nature as she operates in the common modification of society, the leading, guiding, and governing part;" the best able to protect the weak and the less enlightened; the most capable of resisting the strong and the evil-disposed; the most efficient guardians, therefore, of public liberty; "trained to take a large view of the wide-spread and infinitely diversified combinations of men and affairs in a large society," and " habituated to the greatest degree of vigilance, foresight, and circumspection, in a state of things in which no fault is committed with impunity, and the slightest mistake draws on the most ruinous consequences." *

Of such an aristocracy, if it performs its duties and is worthy of its name, De Tocqueville says, that "It may be compared to a firm and enlightened man, endowed with perennial life." † And "when great multitudes act together, under that discipline of nature," Burke recognises "the voice of the grand chorus of national harmony," which he calls "THE PEOPLE." (Vol. iii, p. 87.)

The leaders of the French Revolution repudiated that "discipline of nature," and inspired the French people with what has become their ruling passion—the love of equality; not equality before the law only, but personal and social equality; a vain desire, productive of unceasing jealousies and disappointments; for "those who attempt to level never equalize." ....
" In all societies, consisting of various descriptions of citizens, some description must be uppermost." The attempt to bring all down to one level, and to keep them there, is an attempt to pervert the natural order of things, and is, therefore, the worst of usurpations." ‡

It was the republican Milton, the friend of Cromwell, who did not hesitate to warn his generation against that error. He wrote that, " If not equal all,

---

* Burke's Works, Vol. iii, pp. 85—87.
† " Un corps aristocratique est un homme ferme et éclairé qui ne meurt point." Vol. ii, ch. 5, ad finem.
‡ Burke, Vol. ii, p. 322, Edit. 1855.

yet free, equally free; for orders and degrees Jar not with liberty, but well consist."* Shakespeare has also said: "Take but degree away, untune that string, And hark what discord follows."† The discord in France, which has lasted for nearly a century, has abated little of its violence. It is exhibited in the instability which has given rise in that country to its many changes; from pure democracy and its excesses to its natural result—military despotism; from imperfect attempts at constitutional government to personal rule; and again, at this day, after disastrous foreign and civil war, and the uninterrupted struggles of irreconcileable parties, to the very lately imminent danger of falling again under the domination of one man. "Thirteen times," says M. Taine, "in eighty years have we demolished one government to replace it by another, and in vain, for we have not yet found what suits us." . . . . "Woe to those, the fundamental principles of whose social life have been shaken, and the equilibrium of whose political system has been overthrown by rude and hasty innovations." (L'Ancien Régime, pp. ii, v.) France has reason to regret that the heedless violence of the Revolution, bearing down the helpless incapacity of the upper classes,

---

* Paradise Lost, Book v.
† Troilus and Cressida, Act i, Scene 3. The passage thus proceeds:—

"Then everything includes itself in power,
Power into will, will into appetite;
And appetite, an universal wolf,
So doubly seconded by will and power,
Must make perforce an universal prey,
And, last, eat up himself."

destroyed the opportunity of forming, out of the materials that then existed, a renovated natural aristocracy, which might by degrees have acquired the wisdom and the power to restore and to preserve the balance of society. The arbitrary law, made general soon after the Revolution, for the compulsory subdivision of inheritances, forbids any such healthy growth and revival. The tree no sooner overtops the undergrowth, than it is headed down to the common level.

APPENDIX B.

(Referred to in Pages 139 and 203.)

THE CHANGE, WITHIN THE LAST FIFTY YEARS, OF THE CONSTITUTIONS OF THE INDIVIDUAL STATES OF THE AMERICAN UNION TO PURE DEMOCRACIES, AND ITS EFFECTS ON THE GENERAL GOVERNMENT.

It is important to note, that the present pure democracy in the United States is of a growth many years subsequent to the establishment of its constitution in 1787.

The great founders of the constitution,—Washington, Madison, Hamilton, and Jay,—interpreted Locke's maxim that "Taxation and Representation should go hand in hand" in a sense very different from that which has been usually assigned to it by the democratic schools of more recent times. By those great and enlightened men it was held to mean that Representation should have some relation to property. It was thus not confined to "either persons or property, numbers or wealth," but it was an admixture of all.* Accordingly, during their generation, and for many years after, in all the States of the Union, "a defined portion of real or personal property was requisite for an elector, and a strong aristocratic element pervaded the constitution as then established." †

The first blow was struck at this principle by President Thomas Jefferson, in 1809, by an attack on the independence of the Judges of the Inferior (*i.e.*, the Circuit and District) Courts of the United States; the second, also by Jefferson, and by President Andrew Jackson in his inaugural address for 1829, by promoting the principle of appointing the Judges in the individual States for a term of years. (Story, §§ 1600—1627, and 1618.) The impulse then given towards democratic changes soon extended to the representation; the effect being that Mr. Justice Kent had to record, in 1844, "the almost entire destruction of all the constitutional checks and Conservative elements, which had been regarded by the framers of the constitution as essential to genuine liberty;" and the constitution was reduced to a pure democracy, based on the principles of Locke and the French Revolution.

Mr. Justice Story, in protesting in his great work against the theory of Locke, that there is such a

---

* Mr. Justice Story's Commentaries on the Constitution of the United States, § 632. Boston, 1833.

† Mr. Justice Kent's Commentaries on the American Constitution, New York, 1844, p. 227; a work of equally high authority to that of Story.

thing as an abstract right to vote, affirms that the idea is traceable to the habit of using the word "right." in a too general sense. The imperfection of language leads to the use of the same word to express " natural right " as to express a " civil right." The latter is a mere creation of law for the time being. He says, "The truth seems to be, that the right of voting, like many other rights, is one which, whether it has a fixed foundation in natural law or not, has always been treated in the practice of nations as a strictly civil right, derived from and regulated by each society according to its own circumstances and interests." (§ 580.)

Story proceeds to show that every State in the Union had, at its formation, acted on this principle. " In the adoption of no state constitution was the assent asked of any but the qualified voters; and who should be the qualified voters had been continually settled and altered by themselves." "From this," he adds, " will be seen how little, even in the most free republican governments, any abstract right of suffrage, or any original indefeasible privilege has been recognised in practice." *

The authors of the "Federalist,"—Mr. Madison, Mr. Hamilton, and Mr. Jay,—the great expounders of the principles on which the American Constitution was based; had great misgivings as to whether it was in the power of human wisdom at once to strike out a

---

* Story, § 581.

political system which should combine the elements of freedom and authority in the measure required to satisfy the highest purposes of civil society. They recognised that good political institutions had hitherto been, "not a creation but a growth;" that "intellect, information, and integrity were essential to carry them through their severe trials;" and they designated the doctrines of pure democracy as "idle theories, which amuse with promises of exemption from the weaknesses and the evils incident to society." * Also the whole scope of the learned work of John Adams (afterwards the second President of the Republic) written in 1787, is to prove that no system of constitutional government can be just or desirable that does not guard against the over-predominance of any one of its elements.† In this he followed the great writers of antiquity, who, to use the words of Burke, "considered an absolute democracy, no less than an absolute monarchy, as the corruption and degeneracy of the sound constitution of a republic." ‡

Mr. Justice Story and Mr. Justice Kent give the means of tracing historically the changes which the constitutions of the individual States, and by consequence that of the United States, have undergone since the establishment of the latter in 1787.

---

* Federalist, No. 6.
† The Defence of the American Constitution. By John Adams. London, 1794. 3 vols.
‡ Burke's Works, Vol. ii, p. 396.

Ten out of the original thirteen colonies received their charters between the years 1619 and 1751. The three others,—New Plymouth (the Pilgrim Fathers, 1629), Rhode Island, and Connecticut,—formed their own constitutions.

The ten "chartered" colonies possessed, from the period of their charters down to their separation from this country by their Declaration of Independence in 1776, forms of government, all of which, with some varieties of detail, bore as strict a resemblance to our own as was possible under the circumstances of a new country. They may all be described as moderate constitutional governments. The governor was the king's representative; the crown also appointed a council acting as a consultative body; the judges were appointed by the governor, and during good behaviour; and the governor had the authority to convene a general assembly of representatives of the freeholders and planters. A defined portion of real or personal property was required for an elector, varying generally from a freehold of forty shillings to a rented tenement of £30 or £40, or the payment of taxes.

The colonists were greatly attached to those institutions. Franklin is represented by Burke as expressing the general sense of his countrymen when he said that "he lamented the separation which he feared was inevitable between Great Britain and her colonies. He spoke of it as an event which gave him the greatest concern. America, he said, would never again see such happy days as she had passed under the protection of England. . . . The Americans were going to lose "the rare and precious advantage" they had derived from the good government they had experienced.*

The admixture of the monarchical, aristocratic, and popular elements which those old institutions contained, and the habits of mind produced by them in their public men, exercised great influence, at the time of the separation from us, in moulding the constitution they adopted.

In the celebrated Declaration of Rights of 1774 it was unanimously resolved: "That the respective Colonies are entitled to the Common Law of England;" . . . . and that their ancestors, at the time of their emigration, were entitled (not to the "rights of man," but) "to all the rights, liberties, and immunities of free and natural-born subjects of the realm of England." Also, in the Constitution of the United States, settled in 1787, there is no trace of the theoretical doctrines of Locke, then in vogue in France. The Preamble of the Constitution is as follows: "We, the people of the United States, in order to form a more perfect union, establish justice, ensure domestic tranquillity, provide for the common defence, promote general welfare, and secure the blessings of liberty to ourselves and our posterity, do ordain and establish this Constitution for the United States of America." Their avowed object was "good government;" to be arrived at,

---

* Burke's Works, Vol. iii, p. 30.

not through the adoption of abstract theories, but by means hitherto recognised as leading to that end, and which form the body of the enactments of their constitution.

Nevertheless, in the early part of this century, those abstract theories began to gain favour, and a strong impulse, as above adverted to, was given to them by President Jefferson (1801—1809), and in 1829, by President Jackson, according to the former of whom, in despite of history and the words of the Declaration of Rights of 1774, the colonists brought with them the "rights of men"—of "expatriated men."

From that date, the progress towards pure democracy has been constant and uniform in all the States. All property qualifications for electors have been abolished gradually throughout the Union, with exceptions too small to affect the general principle.

Between 1801 and 1805 seven States had adopted that course, by altering their old constitutions, which contained the same constitutional checks as the Constitution of the United States.

Kent, in 1844, thus describes this progress: "All the States that had been formed since 1800 had omitted to require any property qualification in an elector, except what may be implied in the requisition of having paid a state or county tax; and even that is not in the constitutions more recently formed or amended, except in the Rhode Island Constitution of 1843." *

---

* Kent's Commentaries, Vol. i, pp. 227—229.

In a book of mine, on The Constitution of the United States compared with our Own (Murray, London, 1854), now out of print, but from which I have taken the facts here used, I carried down the information to that date; the result being, that at that time " the members of the House of Representatives in each individual State, and consequently also the House of Representatives of the United States, were returned by voters having, in twenty-two States, no property qualification at all, and in nine next to none; the remaining two only having. retained any valid qualification." (Page 118.)

Pursuing the inquiry to a date as near to the present time (1881) as the best source of information available permits, I find from The American Encyclopædia, which gives the Constitutions of each State, that the qualification for an elector in thirty-four out of the thirty-eight States is now, as a rule, and with very trifling variations, simply that he must be twenty-one years of age, and must have resided a year in the State, six months in the county, and from ten to sixty days in the electoral district in which he votes. Three States have kept up a semblance of a qualification. In Pennsylvania, a voter, if twenty-two years of age and upwards, must have paid a State or county tax; in Tennessee, he must have paid one dollar a year as a "poll tax," and in Delaware, if under twenty-one, he must, within two years previous to the election, have paid a county tax. Rhode Island demands something more; requiring of a naturalized citizen that he should have resided for a year, and possess a freehold of 134 dollars, or pay a rental of seven dollars; permitting native-born citizens, before two years' residence, to vote on the same qualifications; but if they have resided two years in the State, and six months in the electoral district, they can vote if they have paid one dollar in taxes, or served one day in the militia ; but no person can vote for the imposition of a tax or the expenditure of money, unless he has paid a rate on property valued at 134 dollars.

In all the States the elections are either annual or biennial. As a rule, the members of the State Senates are elected for four years ; their House of Representatives, with very few exceptions, is elected annually. As a rule also, the governor and all the executive officers are elected for two years; in some instances for four years, and in a few for one year.

In Kent's time (1844), the evils which "universal suffrage" and frequent elections had brought with them were thus described : " All officers were elected; all offices were held for short periods ; sudden changes were made in the legislation of the individual States, brought about by the alternate succession of opposite parties to power ; the independence of the judiciary was destroyed by the practice of electing the judges for short periods, instead of during good behaviour, and by paying them illiberal salaries." (Kent, Vol. i, page 450.)

In the principles of this system of government and

their results, are to be recognised the doctrines of democratic absolutism inculcated in the seventeenth century by Hobbes and Locke, and in the nineteenth by Bentham, including especially the distrust of all persons placed in authority, so earnestly encouraged by the latter. According to Hobbes, "The only way for a community to erect a common power to keep all in awe, and to direct their actions to the common benefit is, to confer all their power and strength upon one man or one assembly of men, that may reduce all their wills, by plurality of votes, into one will."* Locke's theories have been already commented on (suprà, page 135). Burke thus formulated them as adopted and acted upon by the leaders of the Revolution in France. "The majority told by the head, of the taxable people of every country, is the perpetual, natural, unceasing, indefeasible sovereign; this majority is perfectly master of the form, as well as of the administration of the state; and the magistrates, under whatever names they are called, are only the functionaries to obey the orders which that majority may make. This is the only natural government; all others are tyranny and usurpation." † In order to reduce this dogma into practice, the republicans in France and in other countries were "to destroy all traces of ancient establishments and form a new commonwealth upon the basis of the

---

* Hobbes's Leviathan, p. 157. See suprà, p. 133.
† Thoughts on French Affairs. Burke's Works, Vol. ii, p. 352.

French 'rights of man.' Monarchy was to disappear; every species of nobility, gentry, church and church establishments was to be abolished; all conditions of men were to be levelled (except where money *must* make a difference) all their priests and all their magistrates being only creatures of election, and pensioners at will." *

Bentham thought to arrive at good government by the assumption that the universal dishonesty of governing bodies could only be kept in check by fear. "As each member of the ruling few not only was placed, but at a short interval is displaceable, by the subject many, what such member sees from first to last is, that any considerable and lasting sacrifice of their happiness to his own is impracticable, and that for every attempt to effect it he would be liable to be punished. He will not, therefore, encounter such risk.†

Under this system of government, the progress of the legislation in the individual States affecting the independence of the judiciary was nearly as rapid and complete as that which abrogated all property qualifications for electors. When Story wrote in 1833, five States had adopted the practice of electing the judges. Eleven years later, Kent enumerated twelve more States, in which all the judges were elected, and all appointed for terms of years varying from two and three to seven and eight, and, in one instance only,

---

* Ibid., page 353.
† Bentham's Constitutional Code for All Nations, 1830. Vol. ix of Works, Edit. 1843, p. 97. See also supra, pp. 199—201.

for as many as twelve years. (Vol. i, page 294.) In 1853, I found that the election of judges and their appointment for short periods prevailed in twenty-two out of the thirty-one States of the Union. In three others the elective principle was adopted, but the term was during good behaviour; and in two others they were appointed for a term of years by the governor. I ascertained, also, that in that year the salaries of the judges in twenty-one States ranged from 1,200 to 2,000 dollars (£250 to £400); in five, from 2,000 to 3,000 dollars; in four, from 3,000 to 6,000 dollars; in California, from 2,000 to 10,000 dollars.

Between 1853 and the present year (1881) some improvement has taken place in the payment of the State judges, and the terms for which they are appointed, but the general principle remains the same. An increase has been made in the amount of the judges' salaries, so that in three only of the thirty-eight States are they now below 2,000 dollars. In eighteen States they are between 3,000 and 5,000. In California they are 6,000; in Massachusetts from 6,000 to 6,500; Nevada 7,000; in Oregon 7,000; and in New York from 7,000 to 7,500 dollars; the lowest being £500, the highest £4,500 a year.

There is also a slight improvement in the modes of appointment. In five States the judges are elected by the legislature; in six they are nominated by the governor and the senate; in two they are nominated by the governor. In the remaining twenty-five they continue to be elected by the people.

Further, in a few States, the term for which the judges are elected or appointed is lengthened. Delaware, Florida, Massachusetts, and Rhode Island, appoint their judges for life; New Hampshire, until the age of 70. In ten other States the term has been slightly raised. In California it has been raised to 12 years; in Virginia and West Virginia to 12, in New York to 14, in Maryland to 15, in Pennsylvania to 15 and 21 years. In the remaining seventeen States the elections range chiefly from 4 to 8 years. Illinois has receded from election by the legislature, and for life, to election by the people for 8 years. Louisiana from a term of 8, to one of 5 years. Texas from appointment by the governor for 6, to election by the people for 4 years.*

Both Story and Kent put forth the full power of their minds in endeavouring to impress upon their countrymen the danger both to public and private interests involved in the great change. They considered that—although the Judges of the Supreme Court were still appointed by the President, and during good behaviour—that principle was seriously menaced by the change that had been adopted in the individual States. Story reminded them that the judiciary had hitherto been a co-ordinate power in the state, since no alteration in the constitution could be made without their sanction; "that its independence was the balance wheel of the constitution;"

---

* The American Almanac for 1881.

... "the only check upon the invasions of faction;" ... "the safeguard of the rights and liberties of the people against the tyranny of majorities." (§ 1621.) And with a view to private interests, even in the individual States, "the standard of good behaviour for the continuance in office of the judicial magistracy, was certainly one of the most valuable of modern improvements in the practice of government; ... and the loss of it was the loss of the best expedient that can be devised in any government to secure a steady, upright, and impartial administration of the laws." (§ 1600.) Kent also laboured with equal force to impress upon his fellow-citizens the conviction, that a secure and independent tenure of the judicial office is one of the cardinal points on which their constitution, their liberties, and even the individual safety of life and property, must always in a great degree depend." (Vol. i, page 443.) The destruction, nevertheless, of that independence went on, in state after state, until it pervaded nearly the whole, as has been above shown; in strange forgetfulness that in the celebrated Declaration of Independence of July the 4th, 1776, one of the principle articles of complaint made against the sovereign of this country was, that "he made judges dependent on his will alone for the tenure of their offices, and the amount and payment of their salaries."*

---

* Professor Lieber, in his work on Civil Liberty and Self-Government (Boston, 1853), devotes a chapter of earnest reasoning in support

The ascendancy of pure democracy in the individual States, gave rise to another great political change in 1829, when General Andrew Jackson became President. During the fifty years from the establishment of the American Constitution up to that period, the appointments to the civil service had been made on the ground of fitness and merit. Washington set the example by refusing a nomination to a friend whom he did not consider qualified for the office, and the first six presidents, Washington, John Adams, Jefferson, Madison, Munro, and John Quincy Adams, strictly acted on the principle of not dismissing a public servant except on substantial grounds. But with the presidency of General Jackson, began a system of dismissal and nomination which has been a deep source of regret to all to whom the reputation of their country is dear. This system, under the name of "the spoils of the victor," gave the whole patronage, both in the individual States and the general government, into the hands of the party which was victorious at the elections. The public mind was misled into adopting it by members of the democratic party, and it was carried into effect by that party rigorously, and without check, for upwards of forty years. It has as yet only partially

---

of the elementary truth that "the immovability of judges is an essential element of civil liberty." He also treated the subject very ably in a letter addressed to the German people in 1848 : " Ueber die Unabhängigkeit der Justiz, oder die Freiheit des Rechts in England und in den Vereinigten Staaten."

yielded, within the last ten years, to the patriotic efforts of an influential portion of the republican party to overthrow it.

The great and numerous public scandals arising out of that system which have been continually brought before the public are well known, as also the loss of efficiency which the public service incurs from the frequent and causeless dismissal of many hundreds of officials, from the highest to the lowest.

When the republican party recovered power in 1871, General Grant introduced competitive examinations for the civil service, but with only limited effect, in consequence of the opposition of Congress. His successor, President Hayes, was able to carry the experiment further by establishing examinations at Washington and New York, the results of which, in promoting "the economy, purity, and efficiency of the public service," have been highly spoken of by several of the heads of departments. And more recently a committee of the senate has published a report (Feb. 1881), strongly condemning the "spoils" system, and recommending the general adoption of the principle of competitive examinations "for securing appointments, employment, and promotion in the subordinate civil service of the United States. It is believed that the late President Garfield would have strenuously supported this action of the senate but for the crime of a disappointed office-seeker. The indignation and sorrow at this event, felt no less in this country than in his own, may be expected to strengthen the hands of those who desire to complete this great reform.

The efforts of the large body now set upon firmly establishing this reform in the appointments to government offices, may, by degrees, be followed by a similar change of opinion in regard to the appointments of a like nature in the several States. And it seems not improbable that it may, in the course of time, lead to the correction of the other great abuse intimately connected with the "spoils" system, namely, "the absorption of the whole machinery of the elections by persons who devote themselves to the occupation of arranging them, of fixing upon and bringing forward the candidates, of creating for them a name and character by means of unceasing eulogies in the public press, of dictating to them their policy, of describing in the most minute details the course which it is expected of them to take on all leading questions before the public, and finally, when the elections have terminated in success, looking for their reward from the various sources within the means of the predominant political party, should their candidate belong to it." (The Constitution of the United States compared with our Own, page 107.) The motives for the great exertions of the professional politicians, the "wire-pullers," would be greatly weakened if their present prospect of distributing and sharing the "spoils" were taken away.

In an article on the "Spoils System in American Politics," in the number of the *Contemporary Review* for October, 1881, the author, Mr. William Clarke, quotes from the Life of Andrew Jackson, by Mr. James Parton, the code of political ethics of Aaron Burr, the prominent leader of the democratic party, whose powers and eloquence infected the party with his unscrupulous notions, and prepared the way for their ascendancy under President Jackson (1829-1837) and his successors. That code contains, among others, these maxims:—" Politics is a game, the prizes of which are offices and contracts;" . . . " fidelity to party is the sole virtue of the politician;" . . . "in all conflicts, a man must adhere to the behests of the majority of his own local organization;" . . . "the end and aim of the professional politician is to keep great men down, and to put little men up. Little men, owing all to the wire-puller, will be guided by him. Great men, having ideas and convictions, are perilous, even as tools." (Page 636.)

It would seem difficult for the democratic advocate of this code to point out what room there is in it for the "rights of man." A higher authority has well said—"When the minority are bound to give way to the majority there is an end to ' the rights of man ' for all those who are outnumbered." (Professor William Smyth. See page 255.)

It is to be hoped that the " Liberal Association of Birmingham," known as the " Birmingham Caucus," with its " Federated Associations " now numbering upwards of a hundred, may not be led by degrees to the adoption of all the principles avowed by their prototypes in the United States. But—inasmuch as the organization of our new domestic institution is based on an open popular election, and a complete hierarchy is created, rising through the committees of the primary wards, the local executive committees, and the management sub-committee, up to the central federation, its council of delegates, and its general committee—the power that can be set in motion must be fully as great as that of the energetic "wire pullers" above described. The temptation, therefore, will be considerable to dictate courses of action to constituencies, to candidates, and to representatives. Should this become general, there can be no other result than the lowering of the character of the representative body; for, according to the sentiments urged by Burke before the electors of Bristol, "Any worthy representative of freemen must himself be free." (Vol. ii of Works, page 130.)

The system of frequent elections, also pointed out by Story and Kent as a disadvantage in the electoral system, was not settled by the framers of the Constitution of the United States without considerable differences of opinion. The practice at the time in the different States varied greatly. Virginia elected its representatives for seven years, North and South Carolina for two years, Connecticut and Rhode Island for six months, and the other States for a year. The resolution ultimately adopted and embodied in Article 1, section 2, of the Constitution was, that " The House of Representatives shall be composed of members chosen every second year by the people of the several States."

The results of this system had had time to develop themselves when Story wrote in 1833. He exhibits them with his usual plainness in §§ 592, 593, and 602—604, of his Commentaries; and he notices, in particular, that the system " operates as a great discouragement upon suitable candidates offering themselves for the public service. They can have little opportunity to establish a solid reputation as statesmen and patriots, when their schemes are liable to be broken in upon by demagogues, who may create injurious suspicions, and even displace them from office, before their measures are fairly tried; and they are apt to grow weary of continued appeals to vindicate their character and conduct at the polls, since success, however transparent, is of such short duration, and confidence is so easily loosened."

It is this frequency of the elections, and the large size of the constituencies scattered over wide areas, that throw the management of the elections into the hands of the professional politicians. It was remarked by Sir G. Cornewall Lewis, in his Dialogue on the Best Form of Government (referred to above in pp. 187, 213), " that the tendency of an election so managed is to exclude men of character and ability, and to bring forward second-rate men. It is a system which necessarily leads to the degradation of the representative character." De Tocqueville had long previously made the same remark from his own observations; and there are few passages in his great work more impressive than that in which he affirms and laments the inferiority of the House of Representatives of the United States to the Senate, in all qualities that command general respect, and give political weight and influence.* In the case of the periodical election to the Presidency, the evils of frequency of election are more conspicuous, and are too well known to require any detailed notice.

It was determined, in 1789, that the number of representatives should be one to every 30,000 of the population. The size of the constituencies increased in 1823 to 40,700, in 1843 to 70,680, in 1863 to 127,381, and in 1873 to 131,427; and the number of the representatives which in 1789 was 65, increased in 1823 to 213, in 1843 to 223, in 1863 to 243, and in 1873 to 292. (American Almanack for 1881.)†

Upon these great changes, the editor of a recent edition of Story's Commentaries makes the following remarks:—"Unfortunately, the experience of the United States has not justified the belief that large districts will always choose men of the greatest wisdom, abilities, and real dignity." (Note to § 675 of Story's Commentaries on the United States, 2 vols. 4th Edit. By T. M. Cooley. Boston, 1873.)

The descent of the government of the United States from the mixed and balanced system established

---

* De la Democratie en Amerique. Par Alexis de Tocqueville. Vol. ii, ch. 5. Edit. 1837.

† From March 1883 the constituencies will be upwards of 135,000, and the representatives 325.

by the constitution to pure democracy, dating, as has been shown, from the Presidency of Andrew Jackson, in 1829, has produced consequences deplored by a large body of the most thoughtful and intelligent of the community.

A work published in 1868 amply illustrates that feeling.* The author informs us that "during the two previous years—probably the most important two years in the history of the United States Government, if we consider all the changes that they brought to pass—his daily duties called him into close intercourse with many of the most active public men of the country; and that he has founded his statements and based his conclusions upon authority which ought to be accepted in England, because no one challenges it in America." He speaks freely of what came under his observation; and it is satisfactory to learn from him that "the Americans do not take offence at a candid and fair discussion of the government under which they live."

Writing so soon after the Civil War of 1862—1865, he was able to note one great additional change in the constitution which that war brought forth—namely, that which has entirely altered the position of the Supreme Court. According to the letter of the constitution, no change could be made in it without the consent of two-thirds of the States; and power was

---

* Eighty Years of Republican Government in the United States. By Louis Jennings. London, Murray, 1868.

given to the Supreme Court to annul any change attempted in any other manner. The conquering States believed themselves to be under the necessity of disfranchising for a time, by their own vote, the whole of the ten States that had been in rebellion; in sweeping away the entire judiciary system of those States; and in placing the blacks at once, as regards voting power and consequent authority, in the position of their former masters. By this and other measures the authority given by the constitution to the Supreme Court, as its guardian, was set aside, and can no longer be said to exist. The framers of the constitution would now scarcely recognise their own work. Another proof is thus given, if any were required, that written constitutions are powerless to restrain the immediate action of any future majority of the legislature carried away by the ideas prevalent at the moment.

The direct consequence of the acts of severity against the whites of the conquered States above mentioned, was a fierce and bloody insurrection of the whites against the blacks, attended with widespread devastation and suffering.

But it is remarkable that, instead of the permanent weakening of the influence of the South in the general government, as expected by the North, a gradual and complete reconciliation has taken place between the two races since their franchises were restored to the whites, and especially within the last few years; in accordance, as it is said, with the character of the whites of the Southern States as "instinctive natural rulers." The surprising fact is accordingly now seen that, by means of the united votes of the whites and blacks of those States and of their sympathizers in the North, the democratic party at the last presidential election very nearly equalled the republican, the great supporters of the war; the votes having been, for General Garfield (rep.), 4,442,950; for General Hancock (dem.), 4,412,950.* In 1868, only 8 States voted for the democratic candidates; in 1876, 17; in 1880, 19; being exactly the same number that voted for the republican candidate. The Southern States, therefore, without any desire to reverse the great issues of the past, appear likely to regain their past ascendancy in the government of the republic.

The great social results from the adoption of the doctrines of pure democracy, as far as these had shown themselves up to the publication of my book on The Constitution of the United States, in 1854, have been noticed in the foregoing pages. Mr. Jennings brings down the record to 1868.

The details given by Mr. Jennings are full and instructive, and are supported by unquestionable authorities. They can only be briefly touched upon here. Their general purport is, that the degradation of public life, through the great extension of the suffrage during the last fifty years, and through the action of the Caucus system in the hands of the party managers

---

* American Almanac, 1881.

in the elections, and in the Houses of Legislature, both of the individual States and of Congress, is such, that no interests, whether of the rich or the poor, are safe from the influences of the prevailing corruption.

The corruption has its foundation among the great body of the electors. "In every State, in every county, in every town, there is a rallying point for the adherents of each side. The press is active and well supported, the emoluments at the disposal of the party in power flow safely into distant channels, and the man who does his work knows that he is sure of his pay." (Page 160.) It ascends into the State legislature, where it is "so flagrant, that their legislation, and the venality of the legislators, has become a bye-word and a reproach." (Page 122.) It has established itself in the two Houses of Congress. "If seats in the State assemblies are worth a large price, it may be inferred that a seat in the Federal Congress is a still more precious commodity, and in truth the traffic for it scarcely ever ceases." (Page 124.) The same electors who elect to the State legislatures, have in their hands the election to the Federal House of Representatives, and look to the local leaders, at whose dictation they vote, for their share in due time, of the "spoils." Further, in the choice of senators for the Federal Congress, "the State legislatures are often guilty of shameful corruption." (Page 121.) "Once in the senate, a man may serve his country with fearlessness and honour. But the road to the senate is too often paved with gold, and the gold has come out of the pocket of the candidate." (Page 161.)

The general character of the Federal Congress is thus described by Mr. Jennings:—

"It is almost impossible for a man of independent opinions to obtain a seat in Congress. He must be 'endorsed' by a party, and slavishly adopt all the views of that party, or it is useless for him to contest an election. Should any accepted member exhibit an opinion of his own, in opposition to the general party, he is practically driven out of its ranks; he is assailed on all sides with a virulence and unscrupulousness unknown elsewhere; he inevitably fails to receive a future nomination, and thus he loses the next election. Within the walls of the legislature every voice is raised against him, and outside he has to confront the unprincipled assaults of the combined agents of a faction. Few public men in America can long contend in so unequal a struggle. Thus the power of Congress is securely concentrated in the hands of the leaders of the dominant party of the hour, who may be so actuated by personal ambition, or other unworthy motives, as to render them altogether unsafe guides for the nation. The discussions of this conclave are carried on in secret, and the mockery of a deliberative assembly is made complete by the systematic refusal (in the House of Representatives) to allow of full debate upon measures of the most momentous description. They are decided upon in private Caucus, for reasons which the public are not allowed to know; and when they are brought forward in the legislature, by a form of the House of Representatives known as the 'previous question,' which the adherents of the governing party are almost always numerous enough to enforce, discussion is absolutely prevented. Sometimes, no one is allowed to say a word. The minority is not admitted to the Caucus, and in the House a gag is placed upon their mouths. . . . It is true that in the senate there is no power to forbid discussion, but one branch of the legislature, and that the popular branch, submits quietly to a tyranny which is destructive of the true principles of a legislative assembly, and a betrayal of the trusts confided to it by the people." (Pages 83, 84.)

According to an authority "which is never contradicted in America,—John Stuart Mill,"—everybody should be represented, and everybody should be represented equally. The American theory of representation has entirely departed from this standard. "In other systems minorities are at least partially represented, but in the United States they are practically disfranchised. The best educated, highest-minded class in America are unrepresented, not only in Congress, but in the legislatures of their States." . . . "No one can affirm that either property or intellect is adequately represented." (Pages 81, 138—139.) "Year after year there has been a growing conviction in the minds of the wealthy and cultivated classes that they are deprived of the influence which they ought rightfully to exercise in the affairs of the republic, and that they have no protection against the encroachments of the majority." And the question is asked "whether their system does actually place all men on an equality, or whether they have only reversed the ancient injustices of classes." (Pages 76, 129.)

It has often been remarked that "in the United States the people are better than their constitution." To that effect is the following passage which Mr. Jennings quotes (page 176) from Mr. Fisher's work, The Trial of the Constitution (Philadelphia, 1862):—

"The government is below the mental and moral level, even of the masses. Go among them. Talk to the farmer in his field; the blacksmith at his anvil; the carpenter at his bench—even the American labouring man who works for hire in the Northern States—and compare their conversation, so full of good sense and sound feeling, with the ignorance, vulgarity, personality, and narrow partizan spirit of an ordinary Congressional debate, and with the disclosures made by investigating committees. Evidently the mind and moral sentiment of the people are not represented." (Page 347.)

It has also been noticed, and is referred to by Mr. Jennings, that "there is no people that have a higher and purer ideal than the Americans." (Page 176.) The cultivated and the thoughtful compare their government, as they see it, with what they believe it might be, and what they hope it may be in the future. Their ideal they probably inherit from their forefathers, the great contemporaries of Washington, who did their best under the circumstances of the day to bring their work up towards the standard of the men of the 17th century, who, like Milton, yearned for a republic the basis of which could be described in his words: "Who would be free must first be wise and good." It can hardly be an ideal built upon the unsound and exploded theories of Locke and Rousseau, or the perverted conceptions of human nature and of political and moral principle propagated by Bentham, which have unhappily led astray so many in the last two generations. (See suprà, pp. 199—201, 237.)

On such ideals I beg leave to recall the words of one whose enlightened liberalism and large-hearted wisdom gave him a high place in the esteem and regard of his contemporaries—Professor William Smyth.* The following passages represent, in a compressed form, his conclusions as given in the general summary of his three Lectures on America, delivered at Cambridge in 1836 :—

"What then are the foundations of these democratical institutions? They are the perfectibility of man; they are his virtue and his intelligence; they are his pure and enlightened patriotism, supposed to influence him at every moment. These are no trifling virtues to be required from a community, and not very likely to be found. This high democratic hope, this faith in man, is not justified by fact or reasoning.

---

* See p. 244.

"It is not found in practice in America. It is not in accordance with the principles of human nature.

"Our nature is imperfect. Yet governments are to be made secure, and men to be made happy by their faith in the virtues of each other.

"The Almighty did not depend on the higher virtues of the human character for accomplishing the great purposes of our being. He did not depend on the benevolent interest which every exalted mind was to take in the common weal. He added the sense of self-interest, and the desires and passions of men.

"His system is one of mutual dependence and assistance, of reciprocal obedience and control, of diversified elevation and depression, of interchanged offices of kindness and duty. These call forth the virtues, and provide for the welfare of his creatures.

"The good and bad passions of our nature, the mean and the honourable, the selfish and the disinterested, are so mixed, and checked, and harmonized, that the result is favourable.

"Democracy, in its extreme form, neither wants nor wishes for nor understands the value of the decoration of life, its elevations and its honours, the civilities, the courtesies, the interchanged affections and enjoyments which a highly civilized life is competent to afford.

"There are some in this country who appear to wish to bring us down to that level. Were they to succeed, —in England would die the most magnificent spectacle

of a civilized country that the world has ever seen."*
By the visions of democracy it is "doomed to death, though" (let us hope) "fated not to die."†

The defects that have been commented on in the working of the Constitution of the United States, attract the attention of the European observer, chiefly on account of the light they throw on the exaggerated anticipations encouraged by the theorists of the last century, who pronounced that republics were to be not only free from the failings and defects of the old monarchies, but were to establish an ideal unattainable by them.

No such defects, however, can obscure to any impartial mind the grand spectacle that the old British principles of Common Law and local self-government have presented, in their steady progress over the vast area conquered from nature, in the short period of a century and a-half, by the energy and enterprise of the Anglo-Saxon race.

Nor can the tribute of the highest admiration ever be refused to the spirit which determined that the union of their country should not be broken by the

---

* Lectures on History, by William Smyth, Professor of Modern History in the University of Cambridge, 2nd Series, on America. 3 vols. 2nd Edit., 1842. Vol. 3, ad finem.

† Since this book was prepared for the press, a valuable contribution to the recent political history of the United States, written in a liberal and friendly spirit, has appeared in the number of the *Quarterly Review* for Jan., 1882. Its facts and conclusions are in entire accordance with those of Mr. Jennings, as given by him in 1868, with one marked addition,—A reference to the frequency with which wealth is used to procure corrupt decisions from the state judges.

S

Civil War (however opinions may differ as to its having been avoidable by due foresight), or to the noble self-sacrifice that has submitted to the most burdensome taxation to pay off the debt that ensued. Surely such a nation will one day find the means of removing the blots now observable in its political system.

APPENDIX C.

(Referred to in Note to Page 152.)

THE ORIGIN AND GROWTH OF OUR CONSTITUTION, FROM THE EARLIEST RECORDS OF HISTORY.

THE expression of Montesquieu, that "the English Constitution was found in the woods," strikes a note that has often met with a response in this country. Tacitus has exhibited for us, in the woods of Germany, the framework of the political organization which time has compacted and enlarged into our own.

The German nation, occupying in his time the country between the Rhine and the Danube, was then divided, according to the best information he could obtain, into seven tribes. Each had its king, chosen from the royal stock. Their powers were not arbitrary, but limited. Next in order were the chiefs, also chosen and owing their authority to their qualities as guides and leaders of the people in peace and war. They too, had no arbitrary authority, their powers of correction and punishment being subject to the approval of the priesthood, as representing the Divine sanction.

Their assemblies met by summons on certain days. The chiefs alone disposed of smaller matters; on the weightier affairs all deliberated together, and, wherever the ultimate decision rested with the people, the chiefs had the power of joining in the discussion. They sat down armed. The priests commanded, and enforced silence. The king, or a chief, according as age or rank, or fame in war, or eloquence, gave claims to be heard, spoke with a view to persuade, but with no power to command. The people expressed their displeasure by shouts, their assent by a clash of weapons. Anyone could be arraigned before this assembly, and the punishment of death could be inflicted, or other punishments, according to the nature of the offence. In the same assemblies, chiefs were chosen to administer justice through the hamlets and villages, and they were accompanied by a hundred men selected from the people, who gave the aid of their advice and knowledge, and at the same time enforced the decisions.*

This primitive system of government was no invention of the Tribes described by Tacitus. Their forefathers had brought it with them in their wanderings from the remote east. And when, five centuries after Tacitus, the Angles and Saxons had established themselves in this country, their social and political

---

* Tacitus, De Moribus Germanorum, Lib. i, cap. 1—12.

organization are found to be the same. "The polity developed by the German races on British soil, is the purest product of their primitive instinct. . . The institutions of the Saxons of Germany long after the conquest of Britain, were the most perfect exponent of the system which Tacitus saw and described in the Germania. In England, the common germs were developed and ripened with the smallest intermixture of foreign elements."*

A great accession to our exact knowledge of the laws and usages of the Anglo-Saxons was made by the publication, in 1840, of a large mass of documents upon the subject by the Commissioners of Public Records of the Kingdom, and by the collection of the "Codex Diplomaticus oevi Saxonici," by Mr. J. M. Kemble, published in six volumes by the Historical Society of England between 1839 and 1848. To those new sources of information we are indebted for the many valuable works on our early history that have since appeared, conspicuous among which are the Saxons in England, by Mr. Kemble (1849); the History of the Norman Conquest, by Mr. E. A. Freeman (1870); the Constitutional History of England, by Prof. Stubbs (1874); and the Making of England, by Mr. J. R. Green (1881). The more our knowledge extends of those early institutions the more clearly do we discover our own connection with them; and, in the words of Mr. Kemble, "it cannot

---

* Professor Stubbs's Constitutional History, Vol. i, page 11.

be without advantage to us to learn how a state so favoured as ours has set about the great work of constitution, and solved the problem of uniting the completest obedience to law with the greatest amount of individual freedom.*

From the documents above mentioned Kemble gives a long list of the "Witena-gemotes" (meetings of the wise), from Adelberg, King of Kent, A.D. 595, to Edward the Confessor, 1065. "We are thus enabled," he says, "to follow the action of the Saxon parliament from the very creation of the monarchy."

In the Witena-gemote the rudiments are distinctly marked of our limited monarchy, and of the aristocratic and democratic branches of the constitution. The king could do nothing without the consent of the Witan. Earls or lay nobles and the clergy formed the king's council, in which questions afterwards to be submitted to the general meeting were discussed and argued upon.† The commonalty was represented by the Eorldermen and magistrates of the burghs, and the Reeves of the upland or rural townships. The Ceorls (simple freemen) had doubtless a theoretical right to attend, and exercised it in the smaller assemblies of the Mark and the Shire, and also in the Witan when held near their homes. It may be too much to say they had a right to vote, but, after the manner of their ancestors, they freely expressed their

---

* The Saxons in England. By J. M. Kemble. 2 vols. London, 1849. Vol. i, Preface, page vi.

† Freeman, vol. i, page 79.

assent or dissent, which was practically equivalent to a vote.* But when distance, or their occupations, made it inconvenient to them to attend, some of their number accompanied the Reeve to assist the deliberations by their local knowledge, to make "presentations," to give testimony, and perform other acts relating to the administration of justice, to defend their own rights and complain of wrongs.†

The terms "Eorl" and "Ceorl" ("gentle" and "simple," or "esquire" and "yeoman"), form an exhaustive division of the free members of the state.‡

The origin of the Ceorl's right to attend the Gemote of his own Mark (rudely represented by the modern parish or manor) of the Shire, and of the Witan, was the possession of land. "The possession of a certain amount of land in the district was the indispensable condition of enjoying the privileges, and exercising the rights of a freeman." . . . "Even until the latest period, personal property was not reckoned in the distinction of ranks, although land was. No amount of mere chattels, gold, silver, or goods could give the Saxon franchise." . . . "Loss of land entailed loss of condition in England long after the establishment of our present social system."§ This portion of land, usually a "hide" (an amount varying with the quality of the soil, but of sufficient extent to

---

* Ibid., page 99.
† Sir Francis Palgrave's History of the Anglo-Saxon Period. London, 1831. Preface, pp. xvi—xxv ; pp. 3—17. Kemble, vol. ii, 188—194.
‡ Freeman, page 81. § Kemble, Vol. i, p. 88.

support a family), was assigned to the Ceorl at the time of the conquest and appropriation of any new territory.

To the king and the Eorls the largest portions of the conquered land were allotted; to the principal followers the Thanes, large portions, which often enabled the Thane to rise into the rank of Eorl; to the Ceorls the small portions above named.

After these divisions had been made, much of the territory (Folcland) remained unappropriated, and was used in common. By degrees parts of it were cut off with the consent of the Witan, and consigned to the higher clergy—the bishops and abbots—or to corporations under a written instrument, which gave to them the name of Bocland (Bookland).

This, therefore, was the framework of the English community in the Saxon times; the freeman who was the base of the village society; the township which included "a cluster of farmers' homes;" the Eorl and the Thane, holding larger grants of the public land; the Eorls with the clergy forming the king's council; and the king, who, "representing the national life, and having one of his sons associated with him, to mark the hereditary character of the office, entered into the common stock of the historic dignity of kings."

. . . "Royalty was the product of migration and conquest; the result of prowess in war and of the qualities of a civil ruler. The king's power was co-ordinate with, not superior to, his council."* . . .

---

* Stubbs's Constitutional History. Vol. i., pp. 67, 68.

"The life and sovereignty of the settlement was solely in the body of the freemen whose holdings lay round the moot-hill and the sacred tree;" . . . "In the town moot, the community met from time to time for the ordering of the village life and the village industry; the hundred moot, composed of the representatives of the townships within it, made the laws for the hundred; the Folkmoot, or general assembly, was at once the war-host and highest law-court and general parliament of the tribe." . . . "It was here that England learned to be a 'mother of parliaments.'" It was in these tiny knots of husbandmen that men, from whom Englishmen were to spring, learned the worth of public opinion, of public discussion, the worth of the agreement, the "common sense," the general conviction to which discussion leads, and of the laws which derive their force from being expressions of that general conviction. . . . For "talk" is persuasion, and persuasion is force—the one force which can sway freemen to deeds such as those which have made England what she is. The "talk" of the village moot, the strife and judgment of men, giving freely their own rede and setting it freely aside for what they learn to be the wiser rede of other men, is the groundwork of English history.*

This fair fabric of English liberty was greatly marred by the incursions and ravages of the Danes in the ninth and tenth centuries. The consequent

---

* The Making of England. By J. R. Greene, 1881. Pp. 174—194.

distress that fell upon the small freemen drove them to surrender their freeholds to the Thanes. The principle was introduced that each man must have a lord (Hlaford, loaf-giver), but each was permitted to choose his own lord. Before the time of the Norman Conquest the change for the worse in the Ceorl's condition had made much progress; he was fast descending to that of the "villein," the territorial bondsman, inhabiting the "villæ" or farm buildings; making part of the household of his master and having no political rights; or to the scarcely less servile condition of the "Bordarii" or "Cotarii," the small cottagers with a little land attached, and subject to small payments in kind. From this state of villeinage the bondsman had indeed the power of obtaining his enfranchisement; but the progress was slow, and the whole class had not become enfranchised until towards the end of the fifteenth century.†

Simultaneously with this loss of freedom by the Ceorl, the liberties of the classes above him were impaired by the increasing power of the king, which resulted from the union of the small Saxon kingdoms under one ruler (by Egbert in 829), the subsequent Danish wars, and, finally, the Norman Conquest.

Although the laws of Edward the Confessor were confirmed to the Anglo-Saxon people by William the Conqueror four years after the Conquest (in 1070); and frequently, in subsequent reigns, when the king

---

* Kemble. Vol. i, pp. 89—96.

wanted supplies, the spirit in which they were administered was greatly changed. From having a strong admixture of the democratic element they became purely aristocratic, with a vast accession to the regal power. And thus it was until the great statesmen of the thirteenth century, Earl Simon de Montfort and King Edward, fully established the principle of representation. "In so doing they did but bring back the old state of things in another shape ; . . . and the ordinary freeman received, instead of the right of personal attendance at the Witan, the far more valuable right of attendance by his representatives."*

Writs for sending members to Parliament were for the first time issued in 1264 by Earl Simon in the name of King Henry III. By the writ, the sheriff was commanded to send up to Parliament two knights for each shire and two citizens as burgesses for each city or borough.†

The usual object of calling a Parliament in this and many subsequent reigns was to impose taxes. The

---

* Freeman. Vol. i, pp. 69, 100, 102.

Representation in the modern sense was far from being an invention of that day. Kemble gives, on the authority of Pertz (Monumenta II, 361, 362), an ancient instance of the principle of election. In a Witan by the "old Saxons," in the heart of Saxony, twelve men were elected from each village at a certain time of the year, and by each of the three orders, and formed the general council for the purpose of discussing, passing, and promulgating laws for the common good. "Statuto quoque tempore anni, semel ex singulis pagis, atque ab iisdem ordinibus tripartitis, singillatim duodecem electi, et in unum collecti, in mediâ Saxoniâ secus flumen Wiseram et locum Marklo nuncupatum, exercebant generale concilium, tradentes, sancientes et propalantes, communis commoda utilitatis, juxta placitum a se statutæ legis."

† Hallam's Middle Ages. Vol. ii, p. 148. Edit. 1841. Stubbs's Constitutional History. Vol. ii, p. 222.

earls, barons, and knights of the shire appeared as one body, the clergy as another, and the citizens and burgesses as a third (sitting possibly, as Hallam conjectures, in different parts of Westminster Hall), and each voted such a proportionate tax as they thought fit—an eleventh, a tenth, or sixth.*

The point of time when the knights of the shire were joined in the same house with the representatives of the citizens and burgesses is not, according to the same authority, easy to define, but they were so without doubt in the first year of Edward III (1327).†

In the following reign of Richard II, three great constitutional principles were asserted which firmly established for all future times, in spite of temporary checks and obstructions, the power of the House of Commons—namely, that money could not be levied or laws enacted, without its consent, and that the administration of government should be subject to its inspection and control.‡ And this was shortly afterwards followed by the assertion of the power of the Commons to make supplies depend on the redress of grievances, to punish bad ministers, and to maintain inviolate their own immunities and privileges.§

To the above liberties and privileges the Long Parliament, which assembled in November, 1640, added, in the first nine months of its existence, the great enactments for the periodical assembling of

---

* Hallam. Ibid., p. 169.   † Ibid., p. 170.
‡ Hallam's Middle Ages, Vol. ii, p. 215.   § Ibid., p, 216.

Parliaments, for the abolition of ship money, for restraining the prerogative from levying customs on merchandise, and for the abolition of the Star Chamber; and thus, by the summer of 1641, "formed our constitution, such nearly as it now exists." *

What class or classes in the counties possessed the right of franchise, has been the subject of much discussion. According to some authorities, it was confined to the military tenants holding direct from the king. Hallam was of opinion that as the language of the writs was large enough to include all freeholders, and as the sums payable as wages to the knights of the shire for their services, were levied upon all, the right of electing knights was in all the freeholders who resorted to the county court.† He believed also that gradually, "all persons whatever, present at the county court, were declared capable of voting for the knight of their shire; an opinion which he thought acquired some degree of confirmation from the Statute 8 Hen. VI, c. 7 (1430), which, reciting that elections of knights of shires have now of late been made by very great, outrageous, and excessive number of people dwelling within the same counties, of which most part was people of small substance and of no value, confines the elective franchise to freeholders of lands and tenements to the value of forty shillings."‡

---

* Hallam's Constitutional History, Vol. i, pp. 515—521.
† Hallam's Middle Ages, Vol. ii, pp. 148—152.
‡ Hallam's Middle Ages, Vol. ii, page 243. About that period, although the price of corn often greatly varied, 40s. may have purchased from four to five quarters of wheat, reckoning wheat at from 8s. to 10s. the quarter. When it fell below 6s. 8d. the quarter,

In regard to the original right of franchise in the boroughs, Hallam's view is that those who participated in the liberties of a borough, and were subjected to its burdens, had by a common law right, springing from ancient usage, the privilege of voting at elections. The burgess, at first a free inhabitant householder in the borough holding his tenement in fee; afterwards, if only a lessee of a dwelling for a year, or possessing moveable estate, was liable to the local taxes, and those imposed by the king; and by reason of that liability he had the right of voting.* The process was, that on receiving the writ requiring the election to be made, the sheriff issued his precept to the mayors, bailiffs, and head officers " of every city, town corporate, borough, or such places as have been accustomed to send burgesses according to the old custom and usage;" and although in the incorporated boroughs the elections were, in Hallam's opinion, "for the most part very closely managed in the sixteenth century, and probably much earlier, by the Aldermen and Common Council" (as they continued to be down to the Reform Act of 1832), in all the rest the election was made by the freeholders, or by the inhabitants who were resident householders.†

The writs were sent to all the towns, large and

---

the Statute 15 Hen. VI, c. 2, made perpetual by the 23 Hen. VI, c. 5, (1445), allowed corn "being of small price, to be carried forth of the realm," "si souvent . . . que un quartr de frument n'excede pas le price vjs. viii*d*."

* Hallam's Constitutional History, Vol. ii, p. 200—210.
† Ibid., p. 209.

small, with the exception of those which, by the partiality of the sheriff, were omitted on account of their wish to escape the burden of sending members. Incorporated towns often received the privilege in the hope of profiting by it by increased trade or influence. Thus the representation of boroughs, originating in an act of the prerogative, deprecated sometimes as a burden, and growing into an advantage, gradually began to be claimed as a privilege, and ultimately as a right.

The frequent changes which the borough representation went through from the time of Henry VIII to the Restoration need not here be minutely described. It is sufficient to notice that to the 100 boroughs existing at the time of Edward I,* 33 were added by Charter by Henry VIII, 14 created and 10 restored by Edward VI, 21 created by Mary, 60 by Elizabeth, and 27 by James I. These additions after the reign of Henry VIII were made, not in reference to any popular principle, but "to secure the authority of government, especially in the successive revolutions of religion."† But in the reign of James I, a principle was laid down in favour of popular rights, that "every town which had at any time sent members to Parliament, was entitled to a writ as a matter of course." Accordingly, 15 more boroughs were enfranchised down to the year 1641. In 1673, the county and city of Durham were also enfranchised, having been omitted when the large

---

* Ibid., Vol. ii, p. 209, note. † Ibid., p. 203.

extensions of the right of election were made by Henry VIII, on account probably of the attachment of that part of the country to Popery. In 1677, the town of Newark was enfranchised by Charter, and although this exercise of the royal prerogative was recognised by a vote of the House of Commons, it is the last instance of its exercise that has occurred.*

Nor is a more than a very brief reference required to the continual efforts made by rival parties in the reign of Charles II, and during a great part of the following century, to supplant the ancient right of the resident freeholders by the corrupt agency of small corporations; efforts which were finally frustrated by the Act of 1770, associated with the name of Mr. Grenville, by which the determination of all cases of controverted elections was transferred from the House of Commons to a sworn committee of fifteen members; a jurisdiction transferred in 1868 to the Courts of Law.

But it was not until 1832 that the abuses that had gathered round the constitution during the previous century could be effectually dealt with. By the Reform Act of that year, a large number of the small and corrupt boroughs were disfranchised, a large addition was made to the constituencies throughout the country, and the franchise was considerably lowered. The Liberal Party carried this first great reform; the second was due to the Conservative Party, who, by the Act of 1867, gave us household suffrage. In the

---

* Ibid., pp. 203—205.

same Act, the independent combination of Liberal and Conservative thought, in both Houses of Parliament, compelled the recognition of the right of minorities in large constituencies to their fair share of the representation. (Page 189.)

The time is near at hand when, whichever party may be in power, the franchise will be conferred on the agricultural householder. And it will be conferred with safety if, while enlarging the basis of electoral power, the superstructure is also duly considered. An extension of the principle of the representation of minorities would aid in giving security to the great historic institutions of the country, which we have derived from a remote Past, and which we may trust to hand down in augmented strength to future generations.

The object of this sketch has been to trace the growth of the main principles of our Constitution, not to go into the details of their application in each succeeding age, which belong to history. It is to those principles that we are indebted for the great fabric of our liberties, civil and religious, which has been in the long course of ages built up, extended and sustained, and which, next to individual character, has been the main element of our greatness as a nation.

It would probably be difficult to find an educated Englishman who has not taken into his mind and heart Tennyson's Ode on Freedom. I nevertheless

T

may be pardoned for introducing it in this place, as it has added the charm of undying poetry to the wisdom which is the legacy of all ages on the subject of the Principles of Government.

> Of old sat Freedom on the heights,
>   The thunders breaking at her feet:
> Above her shook the starry lights:
>   She heard the torrents meet.
>
> There in her place she did rejoice,
>   Self-gather'd in her prophet-mind,
> But fragments of her mighty voice
>   Came rolling on the wind.
>
> Then stept she down thro' town and field
>   To mingle with the human race,
> And part by part to men reveal'd
>   The fulness of her face—
>
> Grave mother of majestic works,
>   From her isle-altar gazing down,
> Who, God-like, grasps the triple forks,
>   And King-like wears the crown:
>
> Her open eyes desire the truth.
>   The wisdom of a thousand years
> Is in them. May perpetual youth
>   Keep dry their light from tears;
>
> That her fair form may stand and shine,
>   Make bright our days and light our dreams,
> Turning to scorn with lips divine
>   The falsehood of extremes!

www.ingramcontent.com/pod-product-compliance
Lightning Source LLC
Chambersburg PA
CBHW032104230426
43672CB00009B/1636